★ # CHOOSING COURAGE ★

CHOOSING
COURAGE

Inspiring Stories of
What It Means to Be a Hero

PETER COLLIER

PUBLISHED IN COLLABORATION WITH
THE CONGRESSIONAL MEDAL OF HONOR FOUNDATION

ARTISAN
New York

Artisan books are available at special discounts when purchased in bulk for premiums and sales promotions as well as for fund-raising or educational use. Special editions or book excerpts also can be created to specification. For details, contact the Special Sales Director at the address below, or send an e-mail to specialmarkets@workman.com.

Published by Artisan
A division of Workman Publishing Company, Inc.
225 Varick Street
New York, NY 10014-4381
artisanbooks.com

Published simultaneously in Canada by Thomas Allen & Son, Limited.

Library of Congress Cataloging-in-Publication Data
Collier, Peter.
     Choosing courage / Peter Collier.
        pages cm
     Includes bibliographical references and index.
     Audience: Ages 10 and up.
     ISBN 978-1-57965-596-9
     1. Soldiers—United States—Biography—Juvenile literature. 2. Heroes—United States—Biography—Juvenile literature. 3. United States—Armed Forces—Biography—Juvenile literature. 4. Medal of Honor—Biography—Juvenile literature. 5. Military biography—Juvenile literature. I. Title.
     U52.C65 2015
     355.0092'273—dc23   2014036497

Design by Kara Strubel

Printed in Canada
First printing, May 2015

10 9 8 7 6 5 4 3 2 1

ALSO BY PETER COLLIER

Medal of Honor: Portraits of Valor
Beyond the Call of Duty

CONTENTS

★ CHOOSING COURAGE ★

INTRODUCTION

When students are asked who their heroes are, they often mention athletes, singers, film stars, or other performers from popular culture whose lifestyles they envy. In fact, a real *hero* is a special breed—a man or woman who acts on behalf of country, friends, or even strangers despite great risk to his or her own safety; someone who defends a good cause even when it seems no one else agrees; someone who decides to act when others won't and so changes the outcome of a critical situation.

Choosing Courage focuses on civilian and military heroes who have all these qualities—people who have been able to look inside themselves in crisis situations and find courage and selflessness, people who have the ability to think about others before themselves. Chief among them are the soldiers who have received the Medal of Honor, America's highest military award for bravery under enemy fire. As you read about them, you'll probably feel that what each of them did is almost beyond imagining—charging an enemy position in the face of what seemed certain death, organizing a defense against an attack that threatened to completely destroy their unit, falling on a grenade that might have killed their buddies. Yet every one of these people insists that he isn't special or different, just an average guy who saw something that needed to be done and did it.

The Medal of Honor recipients you are going to read about all received military training that gave them confidence in their abilities and allowed them to remain cool under pressure. But training by itself can't create courage and selflessness—the refusal to give up even though the odds seemed stacked against them, the unwillingness to give in to fear,

LEFT: Four soldiers who received the Medal of Honor for bravery in Vietnam, from left: Jack Jacobs (see pages 199–204 for his story), James Sprayberry, Robert Patterson, and Pat Brady.

OPPOSITE: At sixteen, Jack Lucas was so determined to fight for his country that he snuck aboard this troopship, the USS *Deuel*, to fight the Japanese in early 1945. His story is on pages 5–11.

the need to do the "right thing" even if it means losing their own lives. That strength comes from within.

A similar courage is sometimes seen in the actions of civilian heroes, seemingly ordinary people who do extraordinary things in their daily lives to make our world better. Their stories will also amaze you: the schoolteacher who put her body between a disturbed student with a gun and the other students he might injure or kill; the surgeon who travels the world at great personal risk to treat the poor and powerless caught up in bloody civil wars and natural disasters; a security director in one of the Twin Towers at the World Trade Center in New York City hit by terrorists on 9/11 who gave his life trying to make sure that all the people he was responsible for got out of the building alive. The Medal of Honor recipients honor such civilian heroes with special awards, both to recognize their bravery and to encourage others to act with courage and selflessness in times of crisis.

In this book you will also hear firsthand from others: Men who have received the Medal of Honor write about its meaning and how its lessons apply to the crises of daily life; the mother of a soldier who received the medal reflects on his service and his loss; a woman badly wounded in the war in Iraq remembers her experiences and reminds us of the courage of our injured warriors whose wounds, both physical and psychological, continue to affect their lives for years to come.

These people show that courage isn't something you're born with, but rather something you discover within yourself, that quiet voice that tells you to think of others before yourself when the chips are really down.

They demonstrate, too, that courage is contagious. Several of the people in this book were inspired by other medal winners, whose bravery shows what is possible. You may never find yourself in similar situations, but you may discover, like them, that you are capable of doing great things, things you didn't think possible, when you choose courage.

WORLD WAR II

"The Good War"

W orld War II was seen as a battle of good against evil. Because the good, represented by the United States, Great Britain, France, Canada, Russia, and other nations dedicated to fighting tyranny and oppression, emerged victorious, it is often referred to as the "good war."

Most historians date the beginning of the war to September 1, 1939, when dictator Adolph Hitler, Germany's head of state, ordered his country's armies to invade Poland and declared war against Great Britain and France. Within a year, Germany controlled most of western and central Europe, including France; Great Britain was the only democracy continuing the fight against the Germans. In 1940 Germany formed a military alliance with Japan and Italy, called the Axis, and extended its reach from Europe to the Pacific Ocean. The United States and Great Britain, and later the Soviet Union, joined forces to oppose the Axis. They were known as the Allies.

Reading Right to Left—FIRST ROW: Britain, Canada, Australia, New Zealand. SECOND ROW: Southern Rhodesia, Newfoundland, South Africa. THIRD ROW: India. FOURTH ROW: The Colonial Empire

Reading Left to Right—FIRST ROW: U.S.A., China, U.S.S.R., Yugoslavia. SECOND ROW: Holland, France, Poland, Czechoslovakia. THIRD ROW: Greece, Norway, Belgium

FREEDOM SHALL PREVAIL!

ABOVE: In a morale-boosting poster, soldiers from the Allied countries—including the United States, Great Britain, and Russia—flank the "V" formed by flags of their nations. The "V" stands for "victory" over Japan and Germany, and over tyranny.

OPPOSITE: Many American soldiers had never left home before being sent to the distant battlefields of Europe. In May 1945, the 92nd Buffalo division of African American soldiers pursued the retreating Germans through Italy's Po River valley.

The day after Pearl Harbor, Americans all over the country saw headlines like this one in their afternoon newspapers. The country was at war!

At first the United States was just a spectator. Many in America believed that their country should stay out of foreign wars, especially in Europe, where more than 50,000 U.S. soldiers had died in combat during World War I. An opposing movement, led by President Franklin D. Roosevelt, believed that America should intervene: that Germany's actions in Europe and the Empire of Japan's actions in the Pacific (beginning with its invasion of China) were wars against all humanity and that America couldn't just stand by and watch.

Then, on December 7, 1941, the Japanese attacked America at Pearl Harbor, in Hawaii. Congress declared war on Japan the next day, and two days later Germany declared war on the United States.

Two Wars in Two Places

The United States had to fight what amounted to two wars—against the Nazis in Europe and against the Japanese in the Pacific. This effort required America to produce the equipment of war—the weapons, ships, tanks, jeeps, bombs, and planes—on a massive scale, and quickly. Everyone was expected to contribute to the war effort. For the first time, large numbers of women entered the workplace, taking vitally important jobs in shipyards and aircraft factories. Kids collected scrap metal, rubber, and other needed materials for the war effort. Gasoline and other essentials were rationed.

The momentum of the war, which had been on the side of the Axis powers in the early months, began to shift in June 1942 when the U.S. fleet defeated the Japanese imperial navy in the Battle of Midway. A few

With so many men signing up to fight, large numbers of women entered the workforce, stepping into traditional male jobs such as welders and riveters. They made the airplanes, jeeps, tanks, guns, and munitions needed for the war effort, such as these 1,000-pound bombs.

months later, American forces invaded North Africa and began the fight against the German army there. The following year Allied forces invaded Italy, which then left the Axis alliance and became neutral. On D-Day—June 6, 1944—U.S., Canadian, and British armies landed on the beaches in Normandy, France, and began to move east toward Germany. Meanwhile, the army of the Soviet Union was approaching Germany from the east. On April 30, 1945, American forces met up with Soviet forces in Berlin, the capital of Germany. Within days, Hitler committed suicide and Germany formally surrendered to the Allies on May 8, 1945.

Peace at a Price

By this time, American forces had destroyed the imperial navy of Japan and rooted out Japanese troops in bloody battles on the Pacific

American aircraft carriers were critical to defeating Japan. Each carrier held fighter planes, bombers, and other aircraft. Folded-wing designs allowed the carriers to maximize the number of planes that could fit on board.

Ocean islands of Guadalcanal, Iwo Jima, and Okinawa. Harry Truman, who became president after Franklin Roosevelt's death in April 1945, was faced with a hard choice: invade the Japanese mainland with the result, his generals told him, of at least 250,000 American casualties, or use the atomic bomb to force the Japanese to surrender. He decided to drop atomic bombs on the Japanese cities of Hiroshima on August 6 and Nagasaki two days later. On August 18, Emperor Hirohito of Japan announced his nation's unconditional surrender.

World War II was the deadliest in human history, claiming the lives of an estimated 60 million people. Of this number, approximately 40 million were civilians who died as a result of repeated bombings of densely populated big cities, such as London, Berlin, Moscow, and Tokyo; of the mass murders of Jews and other minorities; and primarily of widespread disease and famine. After the war ended in 1945, some of the German and Japanese leaders responsible for these mass deaths were accused of war crimes, put on trial, convicted, and in some cases executed.

THE BOY
WHO WENT
TO WAR

**"I did a Superman dive at the grenades.
But I wasn't Superman when I got hit."**

Jack Lucas was desperate to fight for his country. And he got his wish by sneaking onto a troopship headed for combat after deserting his unit at Pearl Harbor. It wasn't the first time he'd broken the rules to get into the war: He joined the Marines at fourteen by lying about his age. He was barely seventeen when he went ashore on Iwo Jima, the Pacific island that would be the scene of one of the most intense battles in the history of the Marine Corps. Twenty-seven men would earn the Medal of Honor for their acts of bravery there; the youngest was Jack Lucas.

Jack was eleven years old when his father, a tobacco farmer in North Carolina, died unexpectedly. He felt abandoned and alone, and became a troublemaker unwilling to accept authority. "My mother couldn't handle me," he admitted later on. "She sent me off to military school."

It was 1940, a time when military school was thought of as the last chance for difficult boys—the final stop before juvenile hall or even prison. Jack's mother enrolled him at Edwards Military Institute in Salemburg, North Carolina. There, Jack became more disciplined. He learned that although some things were beyond his control, such as the death of a parent, he could take charge of things in his day-to-day life. Powerfully built, he competed in wrestling and became the captain of the Edwards football team. Over the next two years, he moved up through the school's military ranks, and by 1941, when the Japanese attacked Pearl Harbor, he was a cadet captain. "When I heard about it, the attack, a cold chill ran down my spine," he remembered years afterward. "I just became obsessed that I had to do something."

Too Young to Join

Although Jack was just thirteen, he tried to volunteer at a marine recruiting station. When he was rejected because of his age, he begged his mother to help him enlist—eighteen was the minimum age for joining the military, but seventeen-year-olds were accepted if they had a parent's permission—promising her that he would finish school after the war was over. But she, too, refused because of his age.

Jack wouldn't give up. "I finally took matters into my own hands and forged my mother's signature on the consent paper," he later admitted. Because he was big for his age—five feet eight and 180 pounds with a fireplug build—the marine corps recruiter believed him when he said he was seventeen and signed him up.

Jack had just turned fourteen when he was ordered to basic training at Parris Island, South Carolina. Marine recruits were going into combat every day, and Jack wanted to be part of the action. But when his unit was finally sent to a staging area in San Francisco, a step closer to the war zone, he was ordered to stay behind and train new recruits. His old rebelliousness returned, and he hopped onto the troop train along with his buddies, even though it meant going absent without leave (AWOL). When he arrived in California, he managed to talk his way out of being punished by convincing his superiors that there had been a clerical error in his orders.

By late 1943, Jack was stationed at Pearl Harbor, Hawaii, still thinking of nothing but getting into combat. At this point in the war, military censors read all the mail that soldiers sent home to make sure that no war secrets were accidentally revealed. In a letter to a girlfriend in North Carolina, Jack mentioned his real age—fifteen by then—and one of the censors reported him. When Jack's commanding officer threatened to send him home, Jack replied that he'd just go enlist in the Army and give it the advantage of all his good marine training! He was allowed to remain in the Marine Corps, but he was removed from his rifle squad and given a job driving a truck because of his age.

Looking for Trouble

Unable to get into the fight against the Japanese, Jack turned all his pent-up energy into fights with other marines and civilians at Pearl Harbor nightclubs and bars. "I had eighteen-inch biceps in those days," he later recalled. "I was so muscled up I could run through a brick wall." He was arrested several times, once for punching a policeman who tried to take him into the station for drinking a case of beer he had stolen. He spent a few days in the marine brig.

Early in 1945, when he saw units of the 5th Marine Division being loaded onto ships headed to battle, Jack decided that he couldn't wait any longer. One morning he got up, grabbed a fresh set of dungaree jeans and his combat boots, told his buddies he was going to war, and left camp. The base declared him a deserter after two weeks and offered a reward for his capture.

Jack recovering from his wounds. He inscribed this photo with a note: "To the sweetest mother in all this world. Loving you, Jack."

During this time, Jack had been a stowaway on the troop carrier USS *Deuel*, hiding under the canvas covering of one of the ship's lifeboats during the day, sleeping on the deck at night, and scrounging food from the sailors and marines on board. The *Deuel* was part of a convoy sailing to Iwo Jima, where some of the fiercest fighting of World War II would soon take place. "I'd never heard of Iwo Jima in my life," Jack said later on. "I just knew I was on the way to war, and that's what I wanted."

The Chance to Fight

Afraid of what would happen if he were found out, Jack finally turned himself in when the troopship was well out to sea. A sympathetic colonel decided that instead of sending him back to Hawaii to be court-martialed, he would allow Jack the only thing he really wanted in the first place—to fight for his country.

Jack turned seventeen at sea on February 14, 1945. Five days later, he hit the beach at Iwo Jima with roughly thirty thousand other marines; close to five thousand were killed or wounded the first day. The Japanese had spent years burrowing deep into the volcanic island to establish artillery positions and machine-gun nests in hidden caves and bunkers.

The day after the invasion, Jack was part of a four-man rifle team advancing through a twisting ravine formed ages earlier by lava flow. They came upon an enemy bunker and destroyed it. They took cover in a nearby trench but found eleven Japanese soldiers waiting for them there; Jack shot two of them before his rifle jammed. As he was frantically trying to clear the weapon, he saw two grenades land in the soft volcanic ash near his buddies. "I hollered to my pals to get out and did a Superman dive at the grenades," he recalled. "But I wasn't Superman when I got hit."

One of the grenades failed to go off, but the explosion of the second one flipped Jack over onto his back and caused gaping wounds on his arm, chest, and thigh. He had internal injuries and was bleeding heavily from the nose, ears, and mouth.

THE BATTLE FOR IWO JIMA

February 19, 1945

First, the U.S. forces bombed the island of Iwo Jima from the air and sea. Then the marines came ashore. They trudged across a bleak landscape of volcanic rock and sand, with nothing—no trees, no rock formations, no buildings—for cover. Men and vehicles moved at a painfully slow pace through the deep, coarse sand as relentless fire from the enemy struck from every direction. The Japanese army, 20,000 men altogether, lay in wait. Over the previous year, they had built up a network of caves, tunnels, and underground fortifications throughout the eight-square-mile island. They were prepared to defend it at all costs, knowing how important the island was to American forces. American B-29 bombers needed a base for conducting air raids on Japan, and crippled bombers needed a safe place to land. To the Japanese, it was a fight to the death. To the marines who stepped ashore on this beach of black volcanic sand, it was the worst kind of hell: being fired at from unseen locations in every direction and from the slopes of Mount Suribachi, with nowhere to go for safety. It took thirty-six days for the marines to capture the island, and at a cost of 19,200 soldiers wounded and 6,800 killed.

One of the most famous photographs in American history: Six Americans raise the flag over Mount Suribachi, the island's highest point. Three of these soldiers were killed in battle over the next several days.

Hurt, but Still Alive

Jack's comrades thought he was dead. When another marine squad came forward, one soldier reached down to take Jack's dog tags, a way of identifying those killed in action. "I kept moving the fingers on my left hand to let somebody know I was still alive," Jack explained later. The soldier saw the fingers twitch and called for a medic. Jack was given a shot of morphine to dull his pain and carried back to the beachhead on a stretcher. From there he was transferred to a hospital ship anchored near shore.

Jack was hospitalized in Guam and then San Francisco, where he underwent several of the twenty-six surgeries he would require over the next few years. He was discharged from the Marines in September 1945. He still had more than 250 pieces of shrapnel in his body, some of them the size of a large pebble, which would set off metal detectors at airports the rest of his life.

The volcanic sand beaches of Iwo Jima became a death trap for many marines who landed there on February 19, 1945. They had virtually no cover as they faced intense fire from dug-in Japanese troops.

On October 5, 1945, Jack was awarded the Medal of Honor by President Harry Truman. At seventeen, he was the youngest soldier to receive it since the Civil War. "I'd rather have one of these than be president of the United States," Truman said as he put the medal around Jack's neck. "Sir, I'll swap you," Jack replied brashly, giving Truman a good laugh.

Promises Kept

As he had promised his mother years earlier when he went off to war as a fourteen-year-old, Jack returned to North Carolina to finish junior high—a ninth-grader wearing the Medal of Honor on the first day of school!

Jack eventually got a college degree and became a successful businessman, but he never lost his wild streak. In 1961, at the age of forty-two, he enlisted as a paratrooper in the 82nd Airborne Division to conquer his fear of heights. On his first training jump, both his main and backup parachutes failed to open. Because he miraculously managed to survive the fall without serious injury, his commanding officer joked that "he was the last man out of the plane and the first man down." Jack made another jump two weeks later.

Until his death at the age of eighty in 2008, Jack continued to be honored for his actions at Iwo Jima. But he was always quick to put the praise he received in perspective: "I didn't go to war for some medal. It was to fight for my country. I don't feel like I'm some big hero or anything like that. The real heroes are the ones who had to give their all, their lives. Don't ever forget that."

When President Harry Truman presented him with the Medal of Honor, Jack was the youngest soldier to receive the award since the Civil War.

THE YOUNGEST SOLDIERS:
Children and Teenagers in Battle

Some see combat as exciting. Some see it as a patriotic duty. But boys have always found a way to get into America's wars.

In the Revolutionary War, boys were an accepted part of the Continental army, serving mainly as drummers. It was an important role because voice commands couldn't be heard above the din of battle, and the various drumbeats called the men to assemble, to charge, and to withdraw. Seven-year-old Nathan Futrell, a drummer with the North Carolina militia, is considered the youngest boy to have served in this war.

In the Civil War, the legal minimum age for service was sixteen, but many boys joined the Army looking for adventure, or because they were orphans or had been abandoned, or because they had to help support their impoverished families with military pay. Johnny Clem was ten when he ran away from home after his mother's death and joined the 22nd Michigan Volunteer Infantry Regiment. He began as a drummer, but he also carried a musket tailored to his size, and in the 1863 Battle of Chickamauga he shot a Confederate colonel. Clem was later captured and put in prison for a short time. By the end of the war, he had become famous throughout the country.

Breaking the Rules

In 1918, Mike Mansfield, a future U.S. senator and ambassador to Japan, lied about his age to enlist in the Navy at the age of fourteen. After serving for the remainder of World War I, he left the Navy at age fifteen and joined the Army. At seventeen, he left the Army for the Marine Corps. He served in all three branches of the military before the age of eighteen!

By World War II the minimum age for service was eighteen (seventeen with a parent's permission). But boys like Jack Lucas still found ways to get around the rules and get into the fight—forging their parents' signatures on permission forms, altering birth certificates, or even changing their names and creating new identities. Around two hundred thousand underage soldiers served in this war; nearly fifty thousand of them were discovered by military authorities and sent home to their families.

Even though the rules were further tightened after World War II, in the middle of the war in Vietnam, Dan Bullock, a fourteen-year-old African American, managed to change his birth certificate to fulfill his lifelong ambition of joining the Marines. He was fifteen when he arrived in Vietnam in May 1969. He was killed a month later at An Hoa Combat Base while trying to resupply his unit when it came under attack.

Improved information technology has made it much more difficult for boys to lie about their age in recent wars in Iraq and Afghanistan. But some continue to try to find a way to get into battle.

Johnny Clem was only twelve years old when he served as a drummer boy in the Union Army during the Civil War. He was wounded twice in battle and became a national legend. He later made the military his career, retiring in 1915 with the rank of brigadier general, the last veteran of the Civil War still on active duty.

★ ★ ★ ★ ★ ★ ★ ★ ★

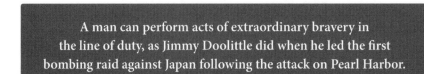

A man can perform acts of extraordinary bravery in
the line of duty, as Jimmy Doolittle did when he led the first
bombing raid against Japan following the attack on Pearl Harbor.
His granddaughter remembers a loving and humble family man.

★ ★ ★ ★ ★ ★ ★ ★ ★

My Grandfather the War Hero

BY JONNA DOOLITTLE HOPPES

For every generation that goes to war, those that follow hear their stories. For many soldiers, the memory of what they did and saw in war is too painful to talk about. Others refuse to glorify themselves for doing their duty. My grandfather, General James H. "Jimmy" Doolittle, never considered himself a hero. He was awarded our nation's highest honor, the Medal of Honor, for leading a bold air strike against Japan barely four months after the bombing of Pearl Harbor. But to those who knew him—his men, his family—he was a giant of a man who taught us that a true hero is kind and generous, curious and loving, decent and fair in all aspects of his life.

★ ★ ★

The plan for the Doolittle Raid on April 18, 1942, called for sixteen B-25 bombers, which were normally land-based, to be loaded onto the aircraft carrier USS *Hornet* and launched within 450 miles of the Japanese coast. The eighty all-volunteer crewmen knew their planes could not

On April 18, 1942, Major General James Doolittle led a flight of sixteen B-25 bombers—the largest planes to take off from aircraft carriers at sea—from the decks of the USS *Hornet* in an attack on Tokyo that shocked the Japanese.

carry enough fuel to make that flight and then return to the carrier. Instead they were going to fly on to airfields controlled by Chinese allies. Unfortunately, the Japanese spotted the carrier when it was 650 miles from the target. My grandfather faced two choices: launch the bombers knowing they might not ever reach the landing fields in China, or call off the mission and push the bombers into the sea so that they would be out of the way of the *Hornet's* regular contingent of fighter planes.

The decision was made: With my grandfather in the lead plane, the B-25s took off from the carrier, knowing they weren't coming back. The Doolittle Raiders almost completely surprised the Japanese when they reached Tokyo. They dropped their bombs, then scrambled for safety. With their fuel running out, all but one of the B-25s' crews were forced to bail out or crash-land. The Japanese captured eight of the airmen and

Major Doolittle poses with a 500-pound bomb, the same type that was used in the surprise raid on Tokyo. The Doolittle raid showed that the United States, badly wounded by the attack on Pearl Harbor four months earlier, intended to fight back.

executed three of them. A fourth died in prison. Three other airmen died in crash landings. The others eventually made it to safety. Their mission had been a success.

The Doolittle Raid did little damage to Japan's mainland. But Japan's military leaders were so shocked by the attack that they withdrew forces from other regions to protect the homeland. Japan was suddenly on the defensive. And American morale, which had been at an all-time low because of the attack on Pearl Harbor, was suddenly on the rise.

By the time my grandfather led the Doolittle Raid, he was already an aviation celebrity—a champion air racer and a pioneering aeronautical engineer and innovator. He not only flew planes, he also designed instruments to help fly them. Growing up in the Doolittle household, though, I was pretty much unaware that the man I knew as Gramps was the famous Jimmy Doolittle. Gramps just played with us and made us laugh. It wasn't until later that I learned about the aviator, the scientist, the general, and a growing respect for the public man was added to the love I already felt for my father's father.

I was always in awe of my grandfather's intellect and his thirst for knowledge. He was forever learning, and it wasn't unusual for him to get up from a family discussion to research the answer to a question. He always read with a dictionary as his sidearm so that he could look up a new word—something he continued to do well into his nineties. To us, he wasn't the hotshot pilot who was selected to lead the famous Doolittle Raid; he was the scientist who earned the first PhD in aeronautical engineering awarded by MIT.

Gramps began serving our country in 1917 when he enlisted in the Army Signal Corps after the United States entered World War I. He would continue to serve, either on active duty or in the reserves, until 1959. He left home to train for the Doolittle Raid in January 1942 and didn't return until after Japan surrendered in 1945. He retired from the Army Air Forces, but

Only one of Doolittle's bombers landed safely. The others crash-landed on or near the Chinese coast. Doolittle (fourth from right) and some of his crew posed with the Chinese soldiers who helped them to safety.

when called on by his country he continued to answer, often as a personal adviser to the president. He impressed on each of us that it was our duty to give back to our country in any way we could.

Over the years, I have had the opportunity to become close with many of the remaining Doolittle Raiders. "What made my grandfather a great leader?" I would ask them. "His word was his bond," they would reply. He was fair, and he led by example, never asking of them anything he wasn't willing to do himself. Gramps led from the front.

In the mess hall, too! A few years ago, I received a letter from a GI who served with my grandfather in Okinawa. The mess hall was a large tent with a water barrel and scrub brush next to the door. After a meal, the enlisted men would line up to wash their mess kits. Senior officers were normally excused from such a mundane chore. But Gramps disagreed. "I met your grandfather standing in line," the GI told me. "I had just washed my mess kit and turned to hand the brush to the guy standing behind me. It was your grandfather. Three stars on his shoulder, waiting his turn to wash his own mess kit." That was typical of the man.

He was fair, and he led by example.

In his autobiography, *I Could Never Be So Lucky Again*, Gramps wrote, "In my nine plus decades, I've formed some views about life and living . . . I have concluded that we were all put on this earth for a purpose. That purpose is to make it, within our capabilities, a better place in which to live. We can do this by painting a picture, writing a poem, building a bridge, protecting the environment, combating prejudice and injustice, and in a thousand other ways. The criterion is this: If a man leaves this earth a better place than he found it, then his life has been worthwhile."

Gramps and his Raiders did just that in 1942. Many of the things Gramps accomplished, from the design of aviation instruments to his leadership of the mission that made him an American hero, have made this world a better place. He passed that purpose in life to us. We, in turn, have passed it to our children and grandchildren.

Like many Medal of Honor recipients, Gramps did not believe he deserved the award. He argued with General Henry "Hap" Arnold (commanding general of the Army Air Forces during the war) and General George Marshall (chief of staff of the U.S. Army) when they told him he would receive the medal. He said he didn't do anything more than any of his Raiders. But the generals disagreed, and they outranked him. When President Roosevelt pinned the Medal of Honor on my grandfather's uniform, he accepted it on behalf of all his boys. And when he walked out of the Oval Office, he vowed to spend the rest of his life trying to earn it.

We all have a gramps or someone we looked up to and who made an indelible impression on our lives. We remember what they did but, more important, we remember who they were.

For his granddaughter Jonna, shown standing at his left in a holiday family photo, Jimmy Doolittle was not so much a national hero but simply her "Gramps"—warm and affectionate, a man of quiet strength whose love of country never dimmed.

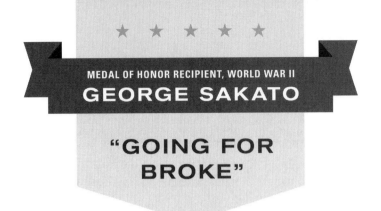

"Do your best and don't put shame on your family."

It was one thing for the German soldiers George Sakato was fighting to regard him as the enemy; after all, he was an American soldier. But it was another thing altogether for George to have been considered the enemy back in his own hometown in California, just because he was a Japanese American. Because of their heritage, Japanese Americans were sent to places called internment camps at the beginning of the war. They were not allowed to leave these camps. It was feared that Japanese Americans would work for Japan—an assumption that proved to be totally false. Yet despite losing his own basic rights at home, George gave everything for the country that had treated him so unfairly.

George grew up in Redlands, California. He was twenty years old and working in his family's small grocery store when the Japanese bombed Pearl Harbor. He was small and slightly built, happy-go-lucky, and always optimistic, but the minute he heard news reports of the attack, he had a feeling of dread. He was a U.S. citizen by birth; his Japanese parents had passed a series of tests to become naturalized American citizens. But George was afraid that because they had been born in Japan, his parents' loyalty to the United States would now be questioned. Their white friends and neighbors stood by them in the days after the attack.

But within two months, the federal government, worried that Japanese Americans might work as spies or saboteurs for Japan, passed laws that took away their basic rights.

Of the nearly 165,000 people of Japanese ancestry living in the United States on December 7, 1941, approximately 110,000 lived on the West Coast. It was there that the government feared a second Japanese attack, and maybe even an invasion, might take place. President Franklin D. Roosevelt issued an executive order that said that Japanese Americans had to move immediately away from the coast to internment camps in remote parts of inland California, Arizona, and other western states. Given only a few days to get ready, many had to sell their homes and businesses at a loss. They were then loaded onto buses and sent to these isolated "relocation centers," where they were crowded into barracks enclosed by wire fences. "These were prison camps with barbed wire fences and guard towers on each corner with machine guns pointing in, not out," George remembered. "It wasn't right. We were Americans."

- BORN 1921, COLTON, CALIFORNIA
- ENLISTED IN U.S. ARMY, 1944
- RANK: PRIVATE
- UNIT: COMPANY E, 442ND REGIMENTAL COMBAT TEAM
- SERVICE AT BIFFONTAINE, FRANCE, 1944
- RECEIVED DISTINGUISHED SERVICE CROSS, 1944, UPGRADED TO MEDAL OF HONOR, 2000, MORE THAN 50 YEARS LATER

Friend or Enemy?

Upset as he was at the way his family and friends were being treated by their own government, George was even angrier at Japan and wanted to fight for the United States. He tried to enlist in the military, but like other Nisei—the name given to second-generation Japanese Americans like George—he wasn't allowed to serve because of his draft status: 4C, which meant "enemy alien."

George Sakato in uniform, about 1944.

Fear about Japanese Americans' patriotism began to grow weaker as the war dragged on, and George was finally able to join early in 1944. He volunteered for the Army Air Force, but when he got to Camp Blanding in Florida, he didn't see any aircraft. "Where are the planes?" he asked. The sergeant who was checking him in answered, "Sorry, you're in the infantry."

George was assigned to the 442nd Regimental Combat Team, a unit made up almost entirely of Japanese Americans. The men, sharing a common ethnic background and also a deep desire to show their love of country, were very close to one another. "We wanted to prove our loyalty," George explained. "We wanted to fight for the United States—do your best and do not put shame on your family. Go to the front and give your life if necessary. When our children grew up, we'd be looked up to rather than down on."

Go for Broke

The 442nd Regimental Combat Team would suffer large numbers of casualties and become the most decorated American military unit in World War II. It called itself the Go for Broke Regiment, using a Hawaiian term meaning "to risk everything." Its war chant began: "Fighting for dear old Uncle Sam. Go for broke! Four forty-two go for broke!"

The U.S. government sent Japanese American soldiers to the war in Europe rather than the one in the Pacific so that they wouldn't have a "conflict of interest" in fighting against "their own people."

In August 1944, two months after D-Day, George arrived in Naples, Italy, where his regiment boarded ships headed to the south of France. After landing near Marseille, the unit began to move up through central France. Its mission was to join other Allied troops moving east from the Normandy beaches in an assault against the German homeland.

Fighting its way north, the 442nd Regiment met the Germans in an intense battle on October 15. As it began, artillery shells rained down on the American forces. The force of a nearby explosion knocked George down. When he picked himself up, he found that another soldier, Yoheie Sagami, had been killed near him.

Later, his unit was entering a wooded area with George on point. Working his way to a curve in the road, he saw a large fallen tree and decided it would be good cover as he looked for snipers in the area. Seeing two fleeing enemy soldiers, he shot at them, but missed. To his surprise, two sets of hands slowly inched up from the other side of the fallen tree holding their weapons over their heads. A sniper and his lieutenant surrendered to him. George took them prisoner, seizing the lieutenant's pistol as a trophy.

Two weeks later, the 442nd approached the French town of Biffontaine, which sat in the mountains near the German border. The Germans had the high ground. "They could see our troop movements a

On December 7, 1941, the USS *Shaw* was one of fifteen major American ships sunk or heavily damaged in a surprise attack by Japanese aircraft on Pearl Harbor.

mile away," George remembered. "They had control of that whole valley. Every time we got into an open area, their machine guns would open up."

Just before midnight on October 28, George's company was ordered to try to get behind the Germans and surprise them. They marched all night; it was so dark that each soldier had to hold on to the backpack of the man in front of him as he moved forward. By dawn, they were in place and ready to storm the German positions. George scrambled up the mountain, working harder than his comrades because of his short legs and because he was carrying a heavy Thompson submachine gun (tommy gun) he had scavenged from a disabled tank.

A Buddy's Death

The Americans succeeded in taking the enemy by surprise. As both sides opened fire, George killed five German soldiers. Then the Germans counterattacked, and the Americans dived for cover. George saw a group of the enemy with machine guns getting ready to fire. He never forgot what happened next: "I yelled, 'Watch for the machine guns up there!' So then my good friend Saburo Tanamachi in the foxhole next to me stood up for some reason and said, 'Where?' And the machine gun shot him. I crawled over to his hole, and I picked him up, and he was trying to say something to me. And then pretty soon, his body went limp, and I knew he died. I sat there and I held him, saying, *Why?* I was so mad. I was crying and I threw off my pack and started a one-man charge up the hill, to get the guys who killed my friend."

> "I threw my pack off and started a one-man charge up the hill, to get the guys who killed my friend."

George fired until his submachine gun was out of ammunition. Then he dropped it and picked up a discarded German rifle. After firing all the bullets in its clip, he opened fire with the pistol he had taken off his German prisoner earlier. In just a few minutes, he killed another seven Germans and led his platoon in capturing thirty-four more.

When the position was secured, George went back down to Saburo's body. In his pocket, he found the 1921 silver dollar his friend carried as a good luck charm—it was minted in the year both he and George were born—and vowed someday to take it home to the Tanamachi family.

A few days after the Biffontaine battle, the 442nd was ordered to go to the rescue of a battalion of the 141st Infantry Regiment—called the Lost Battalion because the U.S. high command was not sure of its exact position. However, it was known to have been cut off by the Germans for several days and was on the verge of being wiped out. The 442nd broke through and rescued the 211 trapped Americans of the Lost Battalion, but at a cost of over eight hundred casualties of its own. At the beginning of this battle, George was hit in his spine and lungs by shrapnel from a mortar shell. The bulky winter overcoat he was carrying in his backpack saved his life, but he was hospitalized for the next eight months.

George was still being treated in a hospital in Washington State a year later when he got a call from his younger brother in California telling him that the local newspaper was reporting that George had been

President Bill Clinton awarded George Sakato the Medal of Honor fifty-six years after his act of bravery in World War II.

awarded the Distinguished Service Cross (DSC), the country's second-highest military medal. What wasn't reported was that George had been recommended for the Medal of Honor but that the award had been downgraded to a DSC.

The gallantry of the 442nd Go for Broke helped change attitudes toward Japanese Americans back in the United States and hastened the closing of the internment centers where they had been taken. But when George and the other veterans returned home, they still encountered bigotry—graffiti that said "No Japs Allowed," restaurants that wouldn't serve them, and other insults—until the mid-1950s, when racial prejudices began to fade.

Making Amends

After the war, George got married and had a family. He worked for the U.S. Postal Service for the next thirty-eight years. In 1999, fifty-five years after that day in Biffontaine where he had lost his best friend, he received a call from the Pentagon. "We want you to come to the White House," the voice on the other end of the line said. "We're upgrading your Distinguished Service Cross to the Medal of Honor."

George was so shocked he couldn't speak.

"Are you there?" the voice finally asked.

"Yeah," George replied.

"I thought you'd had a heart attack," the voice said.

"I almost did," George answered.

The Defense Department had reviewed the actions of Japanese American soldiers during World War II and determined that their bravery had been unfairly ignored or understated. As a result, twenty-two Medals of Honor were retroactively awarded to members of the 442nd Regimental Combat Team. Seven of these men, including George, were still living. His medal was presented to him by President Bill Clinton at the White House on June 21, 2000.

MANZANAR: *Life Inside a Relocation Camp*

Manzanar was the best known of the ten relocation camps where 110,000 Japanese Americans were sent at the beginning of World War II. It was on a desolate and remote 540 acres about two hundred miles northeast of Los Angeles.

By July 1942, seven months after the Japanese attack on Pearl Harbor, ten thousand people were living at Manzanar in thirty-six large wood barracks covered in tar paper. Often, several generations of one family would be assigned tiny apartments no larger than twenty by twenty-four feet. Blankets were used to divide the space into "rooms." Bathrooms were in separate buildings. There were no partitions between the showers and no doors for privacy on the toilets. Kitchens were not included in the apartments. Everyone lined up for meals three times a day in a mess hall to eat army surplus food served on tin pie plates. People who were used to a traditional Japanese diet of fish and vegetables learned to eat Weenie Royales (scrambled powdered eggs and hot dogs) and Spam.

While other American kids went on with their lives, children of Japanese Americans lived behind barbed wire.

Daily Life in Prison

Surrounded by barbed wire with eight watchtowers where armed military police stood guard, Manzanar felt like a prison. But the residents worked hard

Despite hardships, internment camp residents set up schools, social institutions, and even newspapers, including the *Free Press* in Manzanar (right)—where, sadly, no one was actually free. A soldier stands guard (above) to ensure that no one leaves the camp.

to make this situation bearable. They created a "city" inside with its own post office, hospital, churches, graveyard, and schools. (Dozens of teenagers graduated from Manzanar High School during the war years.) They tried to beautify the barren area with rock walls and gardens. They started a camp newspaper, called *The Free Press*, and formed a camp dance band. They set up a baseball league and even built a nine-hole golf course.

The camp residents raised the American flag every morning. Many of the young men who volunteered for the 442nd Regimental Combat Team came from Manzanar.

The camp was closed on November 21, 1945, three months after the war ended. The government gave each resident twenty-five dollars and a one-way ticket to a city of their choice to pick up the pieces of their lives. But many refused to leave because they had nowhere to go, having lost everything when they were first brought to Manzanar itself.

THE
LIFESAVER

"Dear Lord, please let me save just one more."

How can you become a soldier when fighting is forbidden by your religious beliefs? That was what Desmond Doss had to figure out after December 7, 1941, when the Japanese attacked the U.S. naval base at Pearl Harbor, Hawaii.

Desmond was a devout Seventh-Day Adventist, a Protestant denomination distinguished by its observance of Saturday as the Sabbath and its belief in the immediate Second Coming of Jesus Christ. When he was a boy, Desmond's father gave him two framed posters that he kept the rest of his life. One was of the Lord's Prayer. The other was of the Ten Commandments and had an illustration of Cain standing with a club over his dead brother, Abel—the story of mankind's first murder according to the Old Testament book of Genesis. "How could a brother do such a thing?" Desmond asked himself with horror. The illustration profoundly changed his life. "I decided that I wanted to be like Christ— saving life instead of taking life," he said later. He would never kill another human being, whatever the circumstances.

Desmond had just gotten married and was working in the shipyards in Newport News, Virginia, when Pearl Harbor was attacked. Most of the young men he worked with rushed to volunteer for the military. But he

- BORN 1919, LYNCHBURG, VIRGINIA
- DRAFTED INTO U.S. ARMY, 1942
- RANK: PRIVATE FIRST CLASS
- UNIT: MEDICAL DETACHMENT, 307TH
  INFANTRY, 77TH INFANTRY DIVISION
- SERVICE ON OKINAWA, JAPAN, 1945
- RECEIVED MEDAL OF HONOR, 1945
- DIED, 2006

still carried that image of Cain and Abel in his head and imagined God saying to him, "Desmond, if you love me you will not kill." He decided that he would fight in the war, but with a medical kit, not a rifle. He wouldn't take lives; he would help save them.

In every war the United States has fought, there have been people with strong religious convictions like Desmond's who became conscientious objectors—men unwilling to take up arms because of their beliefs. During World War II, a small number who refused to cooperate with the war effort in any way were sent to prison. But most conscientious objectors were willing to serve as long as they weren't forced to carry weapons. Many of them cared for the wounded in hospitals and worked in Civilian Public Service camps established by the government, where they fought fires and did other community projects until the war was over.

Bullied

Desmond signed up as a conscientious objector, but he believed that the war had to be fought and won. Feeling that "it was an honor to serve my God and my country," he joined the Army in the spring of 1942, entering the Medical Corps. During training, other men in Desmond's unit viewed his intense religious beliefs and unwillingness to fight as "weird" and called him a coward. They threw their boots at him when he knelt beside his bunk to pray each night at lights-out, and they bullied him in other ways to get him to fight back. When Desmond refused, they tried to get him transferred. Finally they managed to have him brought before a board of review on charges that he was "unfit for military service." Desmond defended himself, insisting that he wanted to serve: "I'd be a very poor Christian if I accepted a discharge implying that I was mentally off because of my religion," he said. When the review board ruled that he would stay in the Army, Desmond told his accusers that he would be beside them when they went into battle.

Desmond served in the Medical Detachment, 307th Infantry as it entered combat in the Pacific. Carrying only his Bible and his first aid kit, he always volunteered to go on patrols, even when his commanding officer said he didn't have to. "It might not be my duty," Desmond later explained. "But it's what I believed in. I knew these men; if they were hurt, I wanted to be there to take care of them."

And that's what he did. In the summer of 1944, in the middle of a tropical rainstorm during the battle on the island Guam, four Americans were cut down by a Japanese machine gun, and Desmond slogged through

Desmond Doss, at the ready with his medic bag. He single-handedly saved the lives of seventy-five American soldiers before he was wounded by a Japanese sniper.

knee-deep mud to take care of them and drag them back to safety one by one. He received the Bronze Star for this action, and the men in his unit began not only to accept him but also to rely on him. In the bloody battle for Leyte three months later, Desmond immediately rushed out to treat a wounded soldier even though Japanese snipers had him in their sights. For this he received another Bronze Star. The GIs who served with him now understood that it was possible to be very brave as well as deeply religious.

Battle for an Island

In April 1945, the 307th took part in the invasion of Okinawa, a brutal two-month-long struggle that would result in more American casualties than in any other battle in the Pacific. The island was the last stop

Marine medical corpsmen treated wounded American troops at aid stations like this one during the Battle of Okinawa in May 1945.

before an invasion of Japan itself, which made the Japanese soldiers there fight even more fiercely than usual. They had been preparing for battle for months by building networks of storage tunnels, machine-gun nests, booby traps, and camouflaged bunkers on the island.

On May 5, Desmond's unit was ordered to attack a position called the Madea Escarpment, a four-hundred-foot-high ridge overlooking the entire south side of the island, rising straight up the last fifty feet. It was a Saturday—the Sabbath for Seventh-Day Adventists. Normally, Desmond would have observed it as a day of rest, but as his unit pulled out, he reminded himself that Jesus had healed seven days a week, and he went with them.

Desmond's company had fought its way up to the top of the ridge when the Japanese defenders unleashed a savage counterattack including massive artillery, mortar, and machine-gun fire. The Americans were driven back down, leaving dozens of casualties scattered near the top. Desmond alone stayed behind with the wounded.

For the next few hours, protected only by the covering fire of some of his comrades below, Desmond treated one wounded man after another. Enemy machine-gun bullets kicked up dirt all around him, but he moved calmly among the injured, confident that he was in God's hands. He made a rope sling like those he used as a teenager to help rescue people trapped by a flood in his hometown of Lynchburg, Virginia. Then he dragged each man he treated to the edge of the

"I knew these men; if they were hurt, I wanted to be there to take care of them."

ridge, put him in the sling, and lowered him down to the safety of the American position fifty feet below. Each time he got a wounded man down, he returned for another, praying, "Dear Lord, please let me save just one more." By nightfall, he had single-handedly rescued all seventy-five of the wounded who had been left behind on the ridge.

Desmond's explanation for why he had done this was simple: "Because they were my buddies," he said. "And they trusted me. I don't feel like I should value my life above my buddies' lives, so I decided to stay with them and take care of as many as I could."

After many days of hard fighting, the Americans finally took the ridge. Desmond was in a foxhole treating an injured soldier when a grenade landed nearby. He started to kick it away, but he was too late; the grenade exploded, tearing up his leg with shrapnel. He was bleeding heavily, but he insisted that other wounded GIs be evacuated ahead of him. He treated himself, and then waited five hours to be rescued. As he was finally being carried to an aid station on a stretcher, the enemy counterattacked. Desmond gave his stretcher to another injured GI.

Because medics helped soldiers to keep fighting, the enemy always targeted them. As Desmond was slowly limping to the aid station, a sniper shot him. The bullet entered his wrist and traveled upward, lodging in

With the Japanese in bunkers, caves, and tunnels throughout Okinawa—and willing to fight to the death—American troops had to root them out with deadly weapons such as flamethrowers, which were carried or mounted on tanks and projected long streams of fire.

his elbow. He made a splint for his arm from the stock of a rifle—the only time in his entire military service that he carried a weapon.

Desmond eventually dragged himself back to the American lines. In the meantime, some of the men in his unit had gone back to look for him, and when they didn't find him they reported him dead. The news of his death made the front page of his hometown newspaper a few days later. Desmond, now at a field hospital, had a nurse help him write a letter home to let his family know that he was all right.

Honored

Desmond was flown back to the United States for medical treatment. In addition to his arm and leg wounds, he had contracted tuberculosis and would spend the next five years under a doctor's care for his wounds and illness. The only thing he regretted was that his pocket Bible, a gift from his wife that he had carried throughout the war, was lost when he was wounded at Okinawa. But one day, on a visit to the hospital where Desmond was being treated, his commanding officer reached into his pocket and produced the torn, dirty Bible. He told Desmond that after the fighting on the island was over, the men from his company—some of them the same men who had once tried to get Desmond discharged from the Army—had searched the battlefield until they found it. The officer also told him that he was going to receive the Medal of Honor from President Harry Truman. He was the first conscientious objector to be given this award.

After the war, Desmond worked with young people in his church. He was always willing to show them his medal when they asked about it, but he also always made a point of saying that he had received something far more important from his service: "When your buddies come to you and say they owe their lives to you, what better reward can you get than that?"

When President Harry Truman presented the Medal of Honor to Desmond Doss, on October 12, 1945, Desmond was the first conscientious objector ever to receive this award.

★ ★ ★ ★ ★

MEDAL OF HONOR RECIPIENT, WORLD WAR II
VERNON BAKER

FIGHTING FOR DIGNITY

**"I was an angry young man. We were all angry.
But we had a job to do and we did it."**

The cards that life dealt Vernon Baker just kept getting worse as he was growing up in Cheyenne, Wyoming. He was orphaned at age four when his parents were killed in a car accident. His grandparents took him in, but they were so poor that Vernon and his grandfather, a railroad laborer, had to hunt rabbits and other game to put enough food on the table. He was small and skinny, and he kept getting into trouble to "prove himself." His was one of only a dozen black families in town, and he felt the sting of racism every day.

Resentful and bitter, Vernon became such an "unhappy and difficult boy" that when he was ten years old, his grandparents decided they could no longer control him. He was sent to Boys Town, the famous home for delinquent and homeless boys in Omaha, Nebraska. Vernon always credited Boys Town with teaching him the ambition, self-respect, and optimism that allowed him to avoid being defined by anger in the years to come.

★ ★ ★

When he returned to Cheyenne after graduating from high school, the only jobs available to him were shoeshine "boy" and railroad porter. Vernon wanted something more—a career. He decided to join the Army.

· BORN 1919, CHEYENNE, WYOMING
· ENLISTED IN U.S. ARMY, 1941
· RANK: FIRST LIEUTENANT
· UNIT: 370TH REGIMENT, 92ND INFANTRY
  DIVISION
· SERVICE NEAR VIAREGGIO, ITALY, 1945
· RECEIVED DISTINGUISHED SERVICE CROSS,
  1945, UPGRADED TO MEDAL OF HONOR, 1997
· DIED, 2010

It was the spring of 1941. War was raging in Europe and Asia. It seemed unlikely that the United States would become involved, although the military was beginning a slow buildup just in case. As Vernon, now twenty-two, walked into an army recruitment office, he was afraid his size—he was only five feet five—rather than his race might be an issue. He was in for a surprise. "There was this big fat white sergeant sitting behind a desk," Vernon recalled. "'What do you want?' the sergeant asked. 'I'd like to join the Army,' I answered. He looked at me and said, 'We ain't got no quotas for you people.'"

Vernon felt like he had been punched in the face. But after unsuccessfully looking for another job for three months, he tried to volunteer again. This time, there was a different sergeant behind the desk. He signed Vernon up immediately. Vernon didn't know it then, but he would soon prove that good soldiers—and heroes—came in all colors and sizes.

Vernon was assigned to Camp Wolters, Texas, for basic training. When he arrived, racism was waiting for him. Boarding the bus to go from the train station to the army camp, he unthinkingly took a seat near the front. The driver immediately called him the n-word and yelled, "Go to the back of the bus where you belong." He was now part of the segregated military where blacks were generally regarded as "careless, shiftless, and irresponsible," in the words of a report from the U.S. Army War College. They were seen as incapable of serving in combat and requiring "management" at all times by white officers.

First Lieutenant Vernon Baker in uniform, showing his battle ribbons.

That attitude infuriated Vernon: "I was an angry young man. We were all angry. But we had a job to do, and we did it. I knew things would get better."

After basic training, Vernon was awaiting assignment when he overheard a sergeant asking a group of soldiers if any of them could type. Sensing an opportunity, Vernon quickly responded that he could. He was made a clerk and over the next few months worked his way up in rank to sergeant. Because of the initiative he showed, he was among the first black soldiers to attend Officer Candidate School. Early in 1943, he graduated with a commission as a second lieutenant and was assigned to the 92nd Infantry Division, an all-black unit commanded by white senior officers. The men called themselves Buffalo Soldiers, the term the Plains Indians had first used to describe black members of the U.S. Cavalry in the Indian Wars of the 1870s, because of their thick and curly hair.

Early in World War II, black soldiers were assigned to manual labor or supply duties rather than combat. But as the American death toll mounted, things changed. Stationed at Fort Huachuca, Arizona, in the summer of 1943, Vernon heard the chief of staff announce: "All the white boys have been going overseas and getting killed. Now it's time for the black boys to go get killed."

Facing the Enemy

Vernon's unit arrived in Naples, Italy, in June 1944. For the next few months, it pursued the occupying German armies that were now retreating north. One evening, Vernon was on night patrol when he ran into a German sentry. Both began shooting at the same time. Vernon killed the German but was badly wounded in the arm himself. He woke up from surgery a few days later in the segregated ward of an American field hospital and was unable to return to combat for several weeks.

In the spring of 1945, Vernon's unit was near the Italian coastal town of Viareggio. On the cold, rainy morning of April 5, it was ordered to launch a dawn assault against Castle Aghinolfi, a medieval fortress occupied by the Germans that dominated the valley below. Heavily fortified, the castle stood in the way of American efforts to drive the enemy out of Italy once and for all. The steep mountain trails leading up to it had German bunkers, machine-gun nests, and sniper hideouts every few feet. One U.S. battalion after another had attacked the stronghold over the past several weeks, getting cut to pieces each time it tried.

Now Vernon's unit would have its turn. Along with his company commander, a white captain, Vernon led his twenty-five-man black platoon up the mountain just before sunrise. They had reached a shallow ravine about 250 yards below the castle when they sud-

A combat engineer from the 92nd Infantry explodes land mines the Germans had planted on the Viareggio beach in Italy to deter an Allied invasion.

denly encountered heavy German machine-gun and artillery fire. As they took cover, Vernon noticed a telescope pointing out of a slit in an enemy fortification a few feet above him. Realizing that this was an observation post relaying the position of his unit to the guns in the castle above, he crawled up to the slit, stuck his rifle into it, and emptied his clip, killing the two Germans inside. Then he saw two more enemy soldiers firing from a well-camouflaged machine-gun nest nearby and shot them, too.

Vernon was asking for orders from his captain when a German soldier ran forward and tossed a grenade at them. Luckily, it was a dud. Vernon shot the German who had thrown it, then blasted open the fortified entrance of a nearby bunker with his own grenade, killing two more of the enemy.

As the fighting continued, Vernon looked for his captain so they could figure out their next move. He found the terrified officer huddled on the floor of an empty animal pen. The captain said that he had decided to go back down the hill for reinforcements. "I knew he wasn't coming back," Vernon later said. But he agreed to try to hold the position.

> **Vernon ran into a German sentry. Both began shooting at the same time.**

A few hours later, with no reinforcements in sight, Vernon realized his unit had been given up for dead. Nineteen of his men had been killed, and he was wounded in the arm. He decided to evacuate the five others who were still alive. Supported by covering fire from one of his men, he destroyed two enemy machine-gun positions threatening their move, then led his platoon back down the hill to the American lines.

The next day, Vernon volunteered to lead a battalion-sized assault of white soldiers on Castle Aghinolfi. On the way up the hill, he saw the bodies of the men he had lost the day before. All of them were barefoot because the Germans had taken their shoes and socks during the chilly night. Picking their way through minefields and heavy fire, the Americans finally routed the enemy and took the castle.

Life After War

Soon after this battle, the war in Europe ended. Vernon left the Army and stayed in Italy for three years. Then he returned to the United States and reenlisted, making the Army his career, just as he had planned back in 1941. He served in the Airborne until 1968, making his last parachute jump at the age of forty-eight.

By the time of his retirement, Vernon had watched the U.S. military become one of the first American institutions in which blacks could fully participate and had himself commanded units comprised primarily of white soldiers. But he never forgot those brave soldiers he left behind on a remote Italian hillside who died proving how well black men could fight for a country that at that point had not fully accepted them. "Every once in a while I wake up in the middle of the night thinking about those guys," he said nearly sixty years later. "Nineteen souls that gave their all."

More than 125,000 African Americans served overseas in the military during World War II, but none had received one of the more than four hundred Medals of Honor awarded during that conflict. In the early 1990s, an official army inquiry determined that a climate of racism had prevented recognition of heroic deeds above and beyond the call of duty by black servicemen. In March 1996, Vernon Baker got a call from Washington informing him that he was one of seven black soldiers from World War II who were to be retroactively awarded the medal. He was the only one of them still living.

President Bill Clinton placed the Medal of Honor around Vernon's neck on January 13, 1997. Afterward, he was asked what he had learned in his life in the military. His answer was unhesitating: "Give respect before you expect it. Treat people the way they want to be treated. Remember the mission. Set the example. Keep going."

In 1997, President Bill Clinton presented Vernon Baker with the Medal of Honor he had rightly earned— fifty-two years earlier.

BLACKS IN THE MILITARY:
The Road to Integration

After World War II, only one of the Marine Corps' 8,200 officers was African American, and only five of the Navy's forty-five thousand officers. Black political leaders decided to act for racial equality by protesting segregation in the U.S. military.

President Harry Truman also believed the time had come for blacks and whites to serve together. But staff officers from all the branches of the military, including General Omar Bradley, a war hero who was now head of the Joint Chiefs of Staff, were opposed; the Army was "no place for social experiments," Bradley told the president. Congress agreed, saying it was not ready to pass legislation ending segregation.

But the president was prepared to act on his own to end what he thought of as a social evil. On July 26, 1948, he signed Executive Order 9981,

stating that "there shall be equality of treatment and opportunity for all persons in the Armed Services without regard to race, color, religion, or national origin." Truman's order did not take effect overnight, but by the end of the Korean War in 1953, about 95 percent of all units in the military were integrated, and the modern American civil rights movement had begun.

Black servicemen served in specialized—but still segregated—units, such as the U.S. Navy construction engineers known as Seabees during World War II. This unit (above) is practicing landing tactics. The famous all-black 99th Pursuit Squadron, known as the Tuskeegee Airmen because of the Alabama town where they trained, engaged in dramatic dogfights with German pilots over the skies of Europe. Captain Benjamin O. Davis—later the first African American general in the Air Force—reviews his troops (opposite).

THE KOREAN WAR

A Bloody Clash on a Distant Battleground

The Korean War, fought from 1950 to 1953, is sometimes called America's "forgotten war." It wasn't the fight between right and wrong that defined World War II just a few years earlier, and it didn't bitterly divide the American people the way the Vietnam War would a decade later.

Soon after the end of World War II, the alliance between the Communist Soviet Union and the United States and other democracies ended. Taking its place was an undeclared "cold war" that lasted until the Soviet Union began to break apart in 1989. This never developed into a "hot," all-out war on the scale of World War II. But the United States and the Soviet Union, along with their allies, would fight indirectly in places such as Korea and Vietnam in this long conflict between Communism and democracy.

A Nation Split Apart

The groundwork for the Korean War was laid in the final days of World War II, when the Soviet Union declared war against Japan, which had ruled Korea since 1910. The United States agreed that when Japan surrendered, Soviet forces would occupy the northern half of Korea while America occupied the south. On June 25, 1950, North Korea, with superior manpower and with weapons provided by the Soviet Union and Communist China, invaded South Korea. The United Nations condemned this action and authorized the United States and other countries to defend South Korea with military force.

Soldiers from twenty-one countries joined the UN force, but the United States provided 90 percent of the men and almost all of the equipment and weaponry. By the time this force, led by General Douglas MacArthur, entered the war, just weeks after the North Korean invasion, the outnumbered and outgunned South Korean army had been pushed back to the southeastern part of the country. The UN force bolstered the South Koreans, and plans for a counterattack were underway.

OPPOSITE: U.S. Marines endured bitterly cold temperatures in the winter of 1950 as they fought to beat back the Chinese troops entrenched around the Chosin Reservoir in northern Korea.

Chinese troops cross the Yalu River into Korea in October 1950, just four months after the start of the Korean conflict.

From Counterattack to Stalemate

A few months into the war, MacArthur designed a dramatic amphibious landing at Incheon, in the middle of the country. About 75,000 UN soldiers came ashore, liberated the South Korean capital of Seoul, and pursued the North Korean invaders all the way to the Yalu River, North Korea's border with China. The Chinese then sent a massive army across the Yalu that pushed the UN soldiers back into South Korea. The result was a bloody stalemate that lasted for two years.

In July 1951, the two sides began truce talks, which dragged on for the next two years while the fighting continued. A cease-fire was finally signed on July 27, 1953, fixing the border between North and South Korea at exactly the place it had been before North Korea began the war. It also established a 2.5-mile-wide demilitarized zone (DMZ)—a buffer zone between the two sides to help prevent another surprise attack.

The American public was unable to fully understand the reasons for the war—a war that was never declared by Congress and was referred to by President Harry Truman as a "police action." And the outcome—a stalemate rather than a victory—made them want to forget that it ever happened. They didn't fully appreciate the valor of American troops in places such as the Chosin Reservoir, where, in the brutally cold winter of 1950, about 30,000 GIs, surrounded by 67,000 Communist Chinese, inflicted crippling losses on the enemy and broke the siege.

Veterans of America's "forgotten war" could take some consolation in the fact that decades later, South Korea—a nation they had kept from being conquered by Communism—would become a democracy with one of the world's most powerful economies. Communist North Korea, meanwhile, would be reduced to a backward, isolated "hermit kingdom," economically bankrupt and ruled by a brutal and corrupt dictatorship.

General Douglas MacArthur (in leather jacket), the hero of the Pacific campaign during World War II, devised a bold and risky naval invasion to hold back the Chinese army during the Korean War. Although the plan was successful, the headstrong MacArthur would later contradict President Truman's policies and be relieved of his command.

THE
SURVIVOR

"I'm an American, thank God."

Tibor Rubin's fellow soldiers called him Ted, and they loved him because of his bravery. His sergeant called him other names, and he hated Tibor—and even tried to get him killed—because he was a Jew. Tibor's resilience in the face of this anti-Semitism makes his story of survival and heroism through the Holocaust, two wars, and two prison camps, as well as his bravery on the battlefield for his adopted country of America, all the more remarkable.

Tibor Rubin was born in Hungary in 1929 and grew up in a small village called Pásztó. His family was Jewish, but this didn't seem to matter to the other people in town, at least at the time. "We had a beautiful life there," Tibor later recalled about his youth in Pásztó. "We didn't bother anybody, and nobody bothered us."

But then, as World War II approached, the Hungarian government became an ally of Adolf Hitler's Germany and, like Germany's Nazi Party, passed laws limiting Jewish rights: Jews could no longer vote; they couldn't work for the government; they couldn't marry non-Jews; they couldn't teach in schools; they couldn't own their own businesses.

In 1942, Tibor's parents sent him to Budapest, the nation's capital, hoping that he could blend into the big city and escape the violence they feared was coming. He was just thirteen years old. Their fears turned out to be right: Two years later, when the German army occupied Hungary and began rounding up Jews to be sent to concentration camps where they were killed or made into slave laborers, the Hungarian government offered no protection.

Tibor was packed with hundreds of other people into cattle cars and sent to the Mauthausen concentration camp in Austria. When they arrived, the German camp commandant greeted them by saying, "You Jews, none of you are going to get out of here alive."

A Family Is Lost

Years later, Tibor learned what had happened to the rest of his family. His father had been sent to the Buchenwald camp in Germany, where he died. His mother and two sisters were sent to the hellish Auschwitz camp in Poland. When they arrived, the Germans put prisoners in two lines: one for those who would die in the gas chambers, the other for those strong enough to do forced labor. Tibor's younger sister, ten-year-old Elonja, was placed in the first line. His mother, who had been chosen for the second line, ran to be with her. "I'll go with Elonja. She shouldn't have to die alone," she cried out to her older daughter, who was chosen for forced labor and survived to tell Tibor the story.

Malnourished and diseased, Tibor managed to survive until Mauthausen was liberated by the U.S. 11th Armored Division on May 5, 1945. "When they picked me up, I was a sack of bones," he later remembered.

Hungarian-born Tibor Rubin fought for the right to join the U.S. Army.

"I was covered with lice, and it didn't seem that I could live." Fed and clothed and given medical attention, he slowly recovered. The image of American soldiers breaking down the death camp gate stayed with him the rest of his life. "Now I have a debt to pay," he vowed at the time. "I made a promise. If, Lord help me, I ever go to America, I'm gonna become a GI Joe."

In May 1948, after a long wait, Tibor boarded a ship to New York. He was eighteen when he arrived at Ellis Island, the "golden door" where immigrants officially entered the United States. The only clothes he had were the shirt and pants he was wearing—made from U.S. Army blankets. Relief workers sprayed him with DDT to make sure his body was not still infested with lice.

A Jewish refugee organization helped Tibor find a place to live and get a job as an apprentice in a butcher shop in a Hungarian neighborhood in New York City. Everyone spoke Hungarian at work and at home, read Hungarian newspapers, listened to Hungarian music, and ate Hungarian food. It felt like the old country. But Tibor wanted to become an American: "I want to pay back the country that saved me. I decided to join the Army. What was more American than the Army?"

He tried to enlist three times, and three times he failed because his English was so poor. He finally convinced a recruiting sergeant to give him the answers to the language test in advance and managed to pass. He joined the Army in February 1950 and was first assigned to the 8th Cavalry Regiment. Because his name, Tibor, sounded foreign, the other men just called him Ted.

"I Go with the Guys"

Soon after he finished basic training in 1950, the Korean War erupted. Within weeks, Tibor's unit was getting ready to go into battle. As the

Like these Hungarian Jews being transported to the Auschwitz death camp in Poland, Tibor Rubin and his family were facing extermination by the Nazis. Only Tibor and one of his sisters survived the camps.

troops were about to board the ships that would carry them to Korea, Tibor was summoned by his commanding officer and told that because he wasn't a citizen, he didn't have to go into battle.

"What about other guys?" Tibor asked in his broken English.

"They're U.S. citizens, and they're going to fight," the officer told him.

"I go with the guys," Tibor said.

After convincing his commander that he understood and accepted the risks of battle, he boarded a troop carrier ship with the rest of his unit.

Even though Tibor had become close friends with many of the men he served with, he made the harsh discovery that the army that had

(Tibor's story continues on page 54.)

THE HOLOCAUST

When German chancellor Adolf Hitler, the head of Germany's National Socialist Party—the Nazis—plunged the world into World War II in 1939, he set two goals. The first was to conquer Europe. The second was to wipe out all the Jews living there.

Under Nazi rule across Europe, the Star of David was often emblazoned with the word *Jude*—German for "Jew."

Hitler failed to achieve either goal, but for the Jewish people, the cost was staggering. There were about nine million Jews living in Europe at the start of World War II; by the time Germany was finally defeated in 1945, six million of them had been killed in the state-run murder campaign known as the Holocaust.

Anti-Semitism—prejudice against Jews because of their religious beliefs—had been present in Germany and elsewhere in Europe for hundreds of years when Hitler came to power in the mid-1930s. He transformed what had been a deep national prejudice into a homicidal hatred. Hitler claimed that Jews were secretly conspiring to control Germany's economy and culture. He charged that the country's so-called pure Aryan race was being contaminated by the "impurity" of the Jews. He promised the German people that by cleansing the country of the Jewish "pollution," he would make it great again after its defeat in World War I.

The Nazis passed laws denying Jews citizenship, entrance to public schools, and admittance to all professions. Their businesses and personal property were taken. Hitler's brutal secret police, the Gestapo, arrested them and forced them to perform slave labor.

By 1941, with their armies occupying most of Europe, the Nazis had designed a plan for what they called the Final Solution. Jews in Germany, as well as in countries the Nazis had conquered, such as Poland and Hungary,

Jews in Nazi-occupied countries, forced to wear a yellow Star of David on their clothing, were marked for almost certain death.

would be rounded up and killed. The Nazis started by shooting them and burying them in mass graves. But this was too "time-consuming," so they began to transport them by freight trains to death camps whose names would soon become synonymous with human evil: Auschwitz, Buchenwald, Dachau.

There, the Nazis subjected Jews to medical experiments—freezing them to see the effects of extreme cold on the human body, blinding them to study the eye. They herded masses of Jews into gas chambers, where they were "efficiently" killed with cyanide. After the gas had cleared, Jewish slave laborers were sent in to remove gold teeth with pliers and cremate the bodies.

As it became clear that they would be defeated, the Nazis tried to hide evidence of their crimes against the Jews. But when American armies liberated the death camps, General Dwight Eisenhower, commander of the Allied forces, was stunned by the horror of what he saw. He ordered photographers to document the piles of bodies and the starving survivors to make sure that no one could ever deny that the Holocaust had taken place.

liberated him from the Nazis was not free from bigotry. The sergeant in command of his squad hated Jews and repeatedly "volunteered" Tibor for dangerous patrols and missions. Each time Tibor returned from one of them, the sergeant grumbled, "You Jews, nothing can kill you. You're like cats. You've got nine lives."

Tibor ignored the anti-Semitism and did what needed to be done. On one occasion, his unit was fighting near a Korean town called Chirye. When U.S. commanders ordered the company to retreat from a hill it had occupied to a position that could be more easily defended, the sergeant who tormented Tibor ordered him to stay behind, by himself, to cover the movement. Tibor spent the night alone, stocking empty foxholes with grenades, rifles, and ammunition. The next morning, the North Koreans, unaware that he was the only American there, launched an all-out attack on the position. "All hell broke loose," Tibor says. "I was so scared I went bananas. I was screaming."

> **The North Koreans, unaware that he was the only American there, launched an all-out attack on the position.**

Tibor ran from one foxhole to another, firing the weapons he had hidden and lobbing grenades at the hundreds of North Korean soldiers below, making them think they were facing a large force. He single-handedly held the hill until the next day, wounding and killing a large number of enemy soldiers. Then he surprised his sergeant by making his way back to his unit *alive*. Tibor felt that he had proved himself as an individual and as a Jew: "I wanted to show him that we can fight. We bleed like anybody else, and we die like anybody else."

On October 30, 1950, Chinese forces, which had just entered the war on the side of North Korea, attacked Tibor's unit in a massive night assault. Tibor took over a .30 caliber machine gun after three other gunners went down. He continued firing as the rest of the men in his squad retreated. Then he was severely wounded and taken prisoner by the Chinese.

Another Death Camp

Tibor had already survived a Nazi death camp; now he would experience the Communist variety at a place named Pyoktong—called Death Valley by the prisoners. The hundreds of men imprisoned there were cold, hungry, and diseased. Several died each day, mainly from dysentery. Almost as bad as death was the way being imprisoned dehumanized them. "In the front line it is tough," Tibor recalled. "But you are still a free man. When you become captured, you become a nothing. You're no longer a human being."

Tibor used everything he had learned surviving the Holocaust to keep himself and other prisoners alive. Many nights he climbed barbed wire fences and dodged roving spotlights to break into the Chinese supply houses. Jamming whatever provisions he could steal into his pants, he would crawl back to the stockade and give what he had to his fellow prisoners. He treated the sick and injured as well as he could without medicine. When they died, he buried them and prayed over them. The men called him their angel of mercy.

When his Chinese captors found out Tibor was from Hungary—which became a Communist country following World War II—they called him "comrade" and offered to send him back there. He laughed in their faces: "I know what it's like there. I'm an American, thank God."

Tibor was imprisoned in Pyoktong until the end of the war in 1953. The Army credits him with saving more than forty lives during his two and a half years of captivity.

A Medal Is Delayed

Two of Tibor's commanding officers had recommended him for the Medal of Honor for his actions in Korea, but both had been killed, and the sergeant who had displayed such violent anti-Semitism had destroyed all paperwork. But Tibor wasn't thinking about medals when he was released from the prison. He just wanted to get back to America and pick up the pieces of his life. He returned to his work as a butcher and finally received his U.S. citizenship. He married and started a family. He became involved in the welfare of elderly veterans in nursing homes and organized Christmas celebrations for them, becoming known as the "Jewish Santa Claus."

Many of the men in Tibor's original unit believed that he had been killed in action, so they were quite surprised when he showed up at a Korean War veterans' reunion in 1980. When they found out that Tibor knew nothing about being recommended for the Medal of Honor, they contacted the Army and their elected representatives about his case. Partly in response to their actions, Congress passed legislation in 1996 requiring the military to review the records of Jewish American war veterans to determine if any of them had been denied Medals of Honor because of prejudice. Over the next few years, military reviewers who read "Ted" Rubin's file were astonished by what he had achieved.

In September 2005, Tibor was awarded the Medal of Honor by President George W. Bush. He felt very proud, but for him, a refugee from the Holocaust, the best award would always be that he had been able to become a U.S. citizen. "This is the best country in the world," he says. "And

I'm part of it. I don't have to worry if the Nazis are going to knock on my door tonight. Do you understand what this means? I have shalom, peace. People die for it."

President George W. Bush presented Tibor Rubin with the Medal of Honor in 2005, more than fifty years after his ordeal.

A BROTHER
FIGHTS FOR
REVENGE

"I'm going straight up shooting.
It's the only chance we've got."

As the oldest of seventeen children, Ron Rosser learned to take responsibility for others at an early age. "If you bothered one of my brothers, I cleaned your clock," he later said. "And if you bothered one of my sisters, you'd better leave town." In such a large family, he had to learn to take care of himself as well. On visits to his grandparents' farm when he was twelve, he often took a .22 rifle, a backpack with a box of salt and a small skillet, a blanket and a tarpaulin as a bedroll, and disappeared into the nearby forest for a week at a time, living off the rabbits and squirrels he hunted.

Ron's sense of responsibility, his skill with a weapon, and his unshakable courage would one day turn him into a raging, one-man war machine in the frigid hills of Korea, where he would carry out a personal mission of revenge.

Ron's father worked in the mines near the family's hometown of Columbus, Ohio, and everyone assumed that Ron would do the same. But as he later said, "My greatest fear was growing up, getting married, having children, and dying in this same area without a chance to see

Ron Rosser joined up to fight in the Korean War with the main purpose of avenging his brother's death in combat a few years before.

the world." Two of his uncles had served in World War II and had gotten to see the world, so at the age of seventeen he joined the Army and became part of the 82nd Airborne Division.

Growing up in a large family that never had a house big enough for it, Ron had always shared a bed with one of his brothers; in basic training he finally got a bed of his own. He enjoyed training, especially the practice parachute jumps he made, but it was 1946 and the war was over, and he doubted that he would get to jump into a combat situation. He left the Army in 1949 and took a job working with his father in the mines, just as his family always thought he would.

Ron's brother Richard joined the Army in 1950 and was sent to Korea a year later when war erupted there; soon afterward, he was killed in action. Ron immediately reenlisted: "I made up my mind that my brother didn't get a chance to finish his tour, so I was going to finish it for him as a combat soldier," he explained later.

"You Saved My Life!"

Initially stationed in Japan, Ron went to his commanding officer and demanded to be sent into the battle zone. He was soon deployed to Korea as part of the 38th Infantry Regiment. His personal mission was to avenge his brother's death, but he couldn't help being disturbed by the desperate situation of the Korean people: "They had no food. Their homes were gone. Children without families were starving to death." When he saw a U.S. Army cook throw a rock at an orphan boy who was begging for food, Ron forced the man to feed the child and threatened him with a beating if he ever saw him hurt or reject a hungry child again.

· BORN 1929, COLUMBUS, OHIO
· ENLISTED IN U.S. ARMY, 1946, AT AGE 17
· RANK: CORPORAL
· UNIT: HEAVY MORTAR COMPANY, 38TH INFANTRY REGIMENT, 2ND INFANTRY DIVISION
· SERVICE NEAR PONGGILLI, KOREA, 1952
· RECEIVED MEDAL OF HONOR, 1952

Ron went into action as a forward artillery observer, usually alone at some high point in the mountains, observing enemy movements through binoculars and using his radio to direct the fire of U.S. big guns on the enemy below—North Koreans and their Communist Chinese allies—as they massed for an attack. He knew that how well he did his job would determine whether the American lines were overrun. "I didn't know the names of the people I was trying to protect," he said later on. "They were just young soldiers. They knew me, though. One guy came up after a real bad time when the outpost got hit and said, 'Are you the forward observer?' When I said yes, he grabbed me and kissed me and said, 'You saved my life.'"

On January 12, 1952, Ron's infantry company attacked a snow-covered hill (called Hill 472 because it was 472 meters high), where more than five hundred Chinese troops were hiding in an intricate network of trenches they had dug. The enemy was using its superior position to fire down on the Americans—with lethal accuracy. By the time they reached a point about a hundred yards below the top of Hill 472, only 35 of the 170 who had begun the assault were still able to fight. "All the officers were hit," Ron remembers. All the platoon leaders were gone. All the sergeants were gone." What was left of the company was forced to retreat back down the hill.

"All You've Got to Do Is Follow Me"

Ron called the U.S. command center to report the situation, then handed the phone to his captain, who had been wounded in the head and could barely stand. "It was twenty below zero and he had frozen blood all over him," Ron says. "The captain put down the radio and looked up at the mountain and got this real hopeless look on his face." He had been ordered to make a final attempt to take the hill.

Ron looked around at the GIs still able to fight and felt that he had to take responsibility for them, as he had always done for his brothers and sisters. "I'll take them up for you, Captain," he volunteered.

The wounded officer asked Ron what he planned to do. "I'm going straight up shooting," Ron replied. "That's the only chance we've got."

"You know you're not going to make it, don't you?" the captain said.

"Well, we'll try," was Ron's answer.

To the other soldiers still able to fight, Ron said, "If we can get into their trenches, we've got a good chance. All you've got to do is follow me."

As the men gathered behind him, Ron charged up the mountain through the crusty snow, shooting as he went. Bullets from Chinese machine guns came close enough to nip at his uniform, but didn't hit

Family meant everything to Ron Rosser, the oldest of seventeen children. In 1952 his clan gathered to witness him receive the Medal of Honor at the White House.

him. As he reached the first trench, he jammed a new magazine into his carbine and looked back over his shoulder. He was alone. "The other guys were lying all over the mountain where they had gotten hit," he says. "The machine-gun and mortar fire had just cut them to pieces. In the split second that thoughts go through your mind in a life-and-death situation, I got to thinking, 'Well, Ron Rosser, you've come a long way to get here. You might as well make it pay.' So I let out a wild war whoop like an Apache Indian and jumped in the trench with the Chinese."

> **"All the officers were hit. All the platoon leaders were gone. All the sergeants were gone."**

One enemy soldier was directly in front of Ron, another behind him. He shot the first one in the face, then whirled around and killed the other. "The thought of my brother crossed my mind," he later recalled. "This was for him."

Ron fired all thirty rounds in his magazine, killing five more enemy soldiers. He used the stock of his carbine to club another to death while moving toward a bunker where nine more Chinese were hiding. Reloading, he crawled to the top of the bunker, reached down and tossed a grenade into the gun opening, and shot two soldiers who tried to escape after the explosion.

Ron moved to another trench. Chinese soldiers ran toward him firing point-blank. Miraculously, he wasn't hit. He shot several of them, and the rest retreated.

By this time, one of the other GIs had made it up the hill, but as he moved to help Ron, he was seriously wounded by grenade fragments. Out of ammunition, Ron helped the soldier get to the U.S. position about forty yards down the hill. He treated the man's wounds, then stuffed his pockets with ammunition magazines and grenades and plowed back up through the snow to resume his one-man war.

Ron threw a grenade into the first trench he came to, killing several more of the enemy. Then he moved over open ground, firing at every

Howitzers, large guns used to fire artillery shells high into the air for a short distance, were effective against difficult targets such as heavy concrete fortifications.

Chinese soldier in sight. When he had used up all his ammunition again, he went back to resupply, stripping magazines and grenades off the bodies of dead GIs, and returned to fight again.

Getting to Safety

After more than an hour, with the enemy temporarily beaten back, Ron returned to the Americans' position below. Finding that his captain was no longer able to command, he organized a safe withdrawal for what was left of his unit. He made everyone who could still walk take a dead or wounded comrade with him as they struggled back to the U.S. position at the base of the hill.

In addition to getting what was left of his unit to safety, Ron calculated that he had personally killed more than twenty of the enemy with grenades and another twenty-eight with rifle fire. About six months after this action, he was awarded the Medal of Honor by President Harry Truman.

What the Medal Means

In the years since that day in 1952, Ron has often thought about the meaning of what happened on that frozen hill in Korea, when he finally avenged the death of his brother. "When I was young, I was proud of the fact that I killed the enemy," he says. "But as I got older, I was more concerned with the people I saved than the people I killed." When people call him a hero, he shakes his head slowly. "No, to me a hero is maybe an underpaid junior high school teacher who taught in a bad neighborhood all his life and did the very best he could dedicating his life to other people."

Ron has thought about the meaning of the Medal of Honor, too. "A lot of people think that the great thing about the Medal of Honor is that it's awarded by Congress and presented by the president," he says. "But to me, the real honor of the medal is that a handful of young men who were with you at a difficult time thought you were worthy of it."

For his heroic actions in Korea, Ron was chosen to receive the Medal of Honor in 1952. He enjoyed a chat with President Harry Truman after the awards ceremony.

THE SULLIVAN BROTHERS:
One Family's Staggering Loss

The Sullivan brothers (from left to right: Joseph, Francis, Albert, Madison, and George) served together on the USS *Juneau* and were all killed when it was sunk during the Battle of Guadalcanal in November 1942.

Family members have served together in the U.S. military since the American Revolution. And no single family made a greater sacrifice to our nation than the Sullivans of Waterloo, Iowa, in World War II.

The five Sullivan sons—George, twenty-seven; Frank, twenty-six; Joe, twenty-four; Matt, twenty-three; and Al, twenty—enlisted in the Navy after a close friend and the boyfriend of their only sister, Genevieve, was killed at Pearl Harbor. Like Ron Rosser, their motive was revenge. They insisted on serving together, and had to convince a navy recruiter to allow them to do so. All five were assigned to the light cruiser USS *Juneau*.

On November 13, 1942, the *Juneau* was engaged in the Battle of Guadalcanal in the Pacific when it was struck by a torpedo and disabled. A few hours later, as it was heading to a U.S. base for repairs, it was struck by another torpedo. Its ammunition magazines exploded, and the ship sank.

The commanders of two nearby American ships assumed that all hands were killed in the blast and didn't turn back for the *Juneau*. But eight days after the attack, ten survivors were located by an American plane searching the waters where the *Juneau* went down. They reported that Frank, Matt, and Joe Sullivan had died instantly in the blast. Al had survived, but drowned in the shark-infested waters the following day. George lasted for five more days before he slipped over the side of his life raft and disappeared. Some believed that he was too overcome with grief at the loss of his brothers to go on.

Sole Survivor Policy

The Sullivan brothers became national heroes. A naval destroyer, the USS *The Sullivans,* was named after them and went into battle in 1943. (James Sullivan, Al's son, served on board the ship later on.) But to make sure that no other family would suffer a loss as devastating as the Sullivan family's, the U.S. War (later Defense) Department established a "sole survivor" policy three years after the war ended. It allowed servicemen who were the last of a family's children to be taken out of harm's way.

That policy came into play during the war in Afghanistan when Jeremy Wise, a former Navy SEAL who was working for the CIA, was killed in a 2009 suicide bombing. Two years later, his brother Ben, an Army Special Forces combat medic, was killed. The third Wise brother, Beau, serving with the Marines in Afghanistan, was removed from combat and flown home.

Vietnam veteran and Medal of Honor recipient Wesley Fox
reflects on what it really means to be afraid, and how calm,
focused thought and action in times of danger drive away
the soldier's worst enemy, which is fear.

Overcoming Fear

BY WESLEY L. FOX

February 22, 1969, was a miserable, rainy day in the A Shau Valley, South
Vietnam, near the border of Laos. When my rifle company of ninety
marines made contact with a much larger North Vietnamese force that
was lying in wait for us, I couldn't call in air support because of the
weather, and we were too close to the enemy to call in artillery. We were
in a tight spot.

Early in the fight, all of my platoon commanders were killed or
wounded. I was hit by shrapnel from a rocket-propelled grenade but was
still able to lead our badly outnumbered force as the battle developed.
Withdrawal was not an option because it would have exposed my men
to lethal enemy fire.

Later that afternoon, there was a break in the clouds and a couple
of aircraft were able to take out one of the machine-gun positions block-
ing our advance, helping us to turn the tide. In the end, my marines
prevailed despite the loss of twelve good men and fifty-eight seriously
wounded who had to be evacuated by helicopter. More than a hundred

enemy fighters will remain in that valley forever.

I attribute our success on that decisive day to several factors. Motivation played a role. Our lives were on the line, and our only choice was to have the courage to continue the fight. Leadership was important, too: When one of my officers went down, the next ranking marine stepped forward to take charge. And finally, we had been trained to deal with these tough situations and to never give up.

Fear could have been a much more dangerous enemy than the North Vietnamese. I felt it as the fight developed, but I was too busy figuring out what had to be done next and how to do it to let it overwhelm me. The same was true for my men. Although outnumbered, they kept cool and did their job, and fear stayed in the background instead of taking over.

Wesley Fox was a young lieutenant in Vietnam. Here, he uses a field phone to advise headquarters of his situation.

I've known the challenge of fear in other experiences in my life, both in the military and as a civilian. Over the years, I've made 1,198 parachute jumps; in seven of them I had to activate my emergency reserve chute to land on the ground safely. Jump number 797 involved my worst parachute malfunction, and it also rated at the top with the extreme emotions it evoked: stress, concern, and fear for my life. After my main chute failed to open properly, I pulled the reserve chute ripcord, but the suspension lines were twisted from my shoulders to the canopy, and I was in free fall. Fear was knocking loudly on my mental door. I had less than sixty seconds to do something. Somehow, I managed to remind myself: Keep a cool mind, don't

> **I was in free fall. Fear was knocking loudly on my mental door. I had less than sixty seconds to do something.**

rush, and act by the book, one thing at a time. I worked systematically to untwist the lines. I finally freed them, and the chute opened just before I hit the ground. I stood up, hurting all over from the jarring impact but greatly pleased to feel the pain because it meant I was alive.

Another time, I was caught in an ocean riptide while swimming. Fear was beside me as I tried to make it back to shore, but I kept getting swept farther out. I made myself take stock and finally realized that I could make progress only by swimming parallel to the shore and edging toward the beach slowly rather than swimming directly into the riptide. In the end, it still took help from other swimmers to get me to safety.

In these situations, fear was a deadly enemy trying to take my life. I did my best to keep a cool head while recognizing my situation, assessing my options, then taking action, all of which helped me handle my fear. And yes, I was lucky, too.

It doesn't have be a life-threatening situation for fear to be a threat. It is there in the smaller but equally important crises of our daily lives—fear of rejection, fear of being ridiculed, fear of being different. In these

Wesley Fox in uniform, wearing his Medal of Honor.

circumstances, fear paralyzes us and prevents us from coolly assessing the situation we face and doing something about it. If it is not handled properly and promptly, it can and will override common sense, good judgment, and positive decision making. The more we know about how fear affects us, the better able we are to control it.

President Franklin Roosevelt was right when he said, "We have nothing to fear but fear itself." Those with an optimistic outlook tend to react to tough situations more quickly and successfully than those who allow themselves to drown in worry.

American paratroopers were part of the greatest ground-air assault in the Vietnam War. About 700 U.S. troops were dropped behind Viet Cong lines in February 1967.

A commitment to action can also help overcome fear. Calmly figuring out what to do, rather than being scared to do anything at all, can take fear out of a situation and allow us to act with a clear head.

Most important is not to panic and to push fear aside. Once we're out of its shadow, we're free to do the right thing—for ourselves and for others. This is as true for someone overcoming fear in some crucial situation in their daily life as it is for marines in a firefight against an enemy that outnumbers them.

TOM HUDNER

THE COLOR OF FRIENDSHIP

"It was a natural thing for guys in combat to do."

Thomas Hudner and Jesse Brown couldn't have been more different. Tom came from privilege, a white New Englander from a prosperous family who became a carrier-based naval pilot. Jesse came from poverty—a son of Mississippi sharecroppers who grew up in a cabin with no running water, sleeping with his four brothers in a single bed. He too became a carrier-based naval pilot, the country's first African American chosen for duty.

But in 1950, Tom and Jesse would become brothers in combat during the biggest campaign of the Korean War, the battle of the Chosin Reservoir. Only one of them would survive.

★   ★   ★

By the time Tom Hudner graduated from the U.S. Naval Academy in Annapolis, Maryland, and was commissioned as a naval officer in 1946, World War II was over. For the next couple of years, he served on board U.S. warships, but by 1948 he was ready for a new challenge and applied to flight school. He qualified as a naval aviator and was assigned to Fighter Squadron 32 on board the aircraft carrier USS *Leyte*.

The squadron flew the F4U Corsair, a fighter-bomber with distinctive upswept gull wings that had entered service midway through World War II. It was fast and deadly, the American plane most feared by some Japanese pilots, with an 11:1 "kill ratio" during the Pacific campaign.

Tom Hudner (left) in a Corsair F4U fighter-bomber. It was the aircraft that enemy pilots feared the most because of its speed and bombing accuracy. Jesse Brown (above) was the first African American pilot in the U.S. Navy.

By 1950, the Corsair was being made obsolete by a new generation of jet fighters. But when Tom joined Naval Fighter Squadron 32, the plane still had an important mission—providing close support for American ground troops. This mission—making low passes to strafe (fire at) and bomb enemy troops—became especially important when war broke out in Korea in June 1950. After the North Korean army suddenly invaded and overran South Korea, the United Nations Security Council passed a resolution authorizing the UN to get involved. The UN force was led by the United States, which would contribute more than 90 percent of the troops and weapons of the war.

Within four months, this U.S.-led force had pushed the enemy back to the Yalu River, which marked North Korea's border with China. The U.S.-led force seemed on the verge of victory when a large number of Chinese Communist troops unexpectedly invaded, forcing the Americans back and putting them on the defensive.

· BORN 1924, FALL RIVER, MASSACHUSETTS
· COMMISSIONED IN U.S. NAVY, 1946
· RANK: LIEUTENANT JUNIOR GRADE
· UNIT: FIGHTER SQUADRON 32, USS *LEYTE*
· SERVICE AT CHOSIN RESERVOIR, KOREA
· RECEIVED MEDAL OF HONOR, 1951

M HUDNER

By late 1950, about thirty thousand U.S. soldiers were facing nearly seventy thousand Chinese troops in a frozen mountain area known as the Chosin Reservoir. The two-week-long battle there would be the most brutal of the war, and the Americans who survived it would call themselves the Chosin Few after they broke through the Chinese encirclement and inflicted heavy losses on the enemy.

Search and Destroy

On December 4, at the height of the fighting, six Corsairs took off from the *Leyte* on a search-and-destroy mission to bomb and strafe the Chinese soldiers trying to surround the outnumbered Americans. Tom was the pilot of one of these planes, flying as wingman for Jesse. Tom never thought about being an aviator until he spent seven months on a U.S. cruiser, operating between Taiwan and the China coast. Jesse had wanted to fly since the age of six, when his father took him to a local air show. After graduating from a segregated Mississippi high school, Jesse was one of only a few African Americans admitted to Ohio State University, where he paid his way by washing dishes. He joined an aviation cadet program and was accepted for U.S. naval flight training after graduating in 1946. Newspapers and magazines featured photographs of him receiving his wings as the first African American naval aviator in 1947—the same year that Jackie Robinson broke the color barrier in baseball.

As a black man in a white world of pilots and other officers, Jesse experienced a lot of racial taunts in his first days in the Navy. When he embarked with VF-32 on the USS *Leyte* and was introduced to Tom, he didn't extend his hand to shake for fear that he would be rejected. But Tom quickly extended his and shook Jesse's warmly. Tom and the

Jesse Brown, piloting his Corsair F4U fighter-bomber, was shot down over North Korea in 1950. Despite all rescue efforts, he perished at the crash site.

men of Fighter Squadron 32 tried to protect Jesse from the bigotry he encountered—especially on shore leave from the *Leyte*—and they came to respect his ability to coolly handle the prejudice that came along with his celebrity.

The six Corsairs that took off from the carrier deck into the noon-day sun that December 4 had been airborne for about an hour and were skimming low over the frozen mountains around Chosin in search of Chinese Communist troops when Jesse's plane was hit by ground fire. One of the other pilots saw a vapor trail from a ruptured fuel line. As his wingman, Tom had a special responsibility to protect Jesse. Watching the plane rapidly lose altitude, he realized that it was too low for Jesse to bail out and that he would have to ditch. Tom followed the Corsair down, calling off a checklist of information over the radio to help Jesse prepare for a crash landing.

Another pilot in the formation radioed a Mayday alert as Jesse's plane smashed into the heavy snow. Making a pass over the wreckage, Tom at first thought it impossible that Jesse could have survived. But when he flew lower over the damaged Corsair, he saw Jesse open the canopy and wave weakly as he tried to free himself from the cockpit.

"I'm Going In!"

Tom knew that the rescue helicopters had a long way to come and that his injured friend would be helpless until they arrived. He thought to himself, "My God, I've got to make a decision!" Not asking permission because he knew it would be denied, he radioed his flight leader, "I'm going in!" Then he dumped the bombs his plane was still carrying, dropped the wing flaps to reduce his air speed, and went in with his wheels up.

Tom's plane hit hard. He climbed out and tried to clear his head as he struggled through the heavy snow to Jesse's Corsair. At an altitude of six thousand feet, the temperature was near zero although it was early afternoon. (It got as low as thirty below zero in these mountains in the middle of the night in December.) Tom tried to climb up on the wing of Jesse's plane, but it was coated with snow and he kept slipping off. He finally managed to pull himself up. Looking into the cockpit, he saw that Jesse's right leg had been crushed by the damaged instrument panel; he had apparently suffered internal injuries as well.

> "Tom, we're going to have to figure a way to get out of here."

Jesse was barely able to speak. He had taken off his gloves while trying to disentangle himself from his harness, and his hands were already frozen. Tom covered them with his scarf. "Tom, we're going to have to figure a way to get out of here," Jesse said feebly. Tom grabbed him by the shoulders and tried as hard as he could to pull him out of the cockpit. But Jesse's lower body was pinned in and couldn't be budged.

The engine of the wrecked Corsair had begun to smoke, and Tom feared it might catch fire at any moment. He burned his hands when he tried to pack snow on it to keep flames from erupting. As he worked on the engine, he kept talking to Jesse, who was now drifting in and out of consciousness.

It was late afternoon when a U.S. Marine helicopter finally arrived after supporting marines about twenty-five miles away. The pilot used a fire extinguisher to try to cool the Corsair's engine. Then he and Tom hacked at the fuselage with an ax for almost an hour to try to get Jesse free from the wreckage, but it just bounced off the metal.

Tom didn't want to leave his friend behind, but he could see that Jesse was dying. Jesse seemed to realize it, too. His last words, whispered to Tom, were about his wife: "Tell Daisy I love her."

With the sun going down and the cold settling down around them like a blanket, the helicopter pilot told Tom that they would have to act fast because the helicopter couldn't fly in the dangerous mountain area after dark. Reluctantly, Tom left the crash site. "I told Jesse we were going back to get equipment," he recalled. "I don't know if he heard me. I don't know if he was alive at that time."

Jesse Brown's widow, Daisy, shakes the hand of Tom Hudner, the pilot who tried desperately to save her husband in the frozen mountains of North Korea.

When Tom landed back on the *Leyte*, the ship's captain considered ordering a second flight of fighters to escort another helicopter carrying a flight surgeon back to the crash site. But he decided against it, because it would have meant putting too many other men in danger for an uncertain result.

> **One of the pilots recited the Lord's Prayer during the bombing run.**

The next morning, photographs taken by U.S. reconnaissance planes showed that Chinese Communist soldiers had stripped off Jesse's clothing during the night. The ship's captain ordered four Corsairs to fly over the wreckage and drop flaming napalm on the downed plane so that Jesse's body wouldn't be desecrated by the enemy and so that he would at least have a warrior's funeral. One of the pilots recited the Lord's Prayer during the bombing run.

By February 1951, when the *Leyte* arrived back in port in the United States, the incident was still in the news. When journalists questioned Tom about why he had crash-landed his plane to try to save Jesse, he told them, "It was a natural thing for guys in combat to do for shipmates and comrades. If I'd been on the ground, somebody would have done it for me."

A few weeks later, Tom found out that he was to be the first American servicemen in the Korean War to receive the Medal of Honor. Daisy Brown, Jesse's widow, was present as an invited guest when President Harry Truman put the medal around Tom's neck on April 13, 1951. (Jesse would later be posthumously awarded the Distinguished Flying Cross.)

Looking for Jesse

In the coming years, there would be other honors for both men. In 1973, the U.S. Navy commissioned a frigate named the USS *Jesse L. Brown*. In 2012, the Defense Department announced that it was building a new destroyer to be called the USS *Thomas J. Hudner*.

Tom Hudner became the first American serviceman to receive the Medal of Honor for actions in the Korean War. President Truman congratulates Tom as his family looks on.

But Tom never forgot Jesse or the pain of not being able to bring his friend home. In the fall of 2013, at the age of eighty-nine, he embarked on a secret trip to North Korea to look for the site where Jesse had died. It was not clear why the North Korean government, still as tyrannical and unpredictable as it had been during the Korean War, agreed to his visit. But at the last minute, just as Tom was getting ready to trek into the mountains of the Chosin Reservoir where Jesse's Corsair had crashed more than sixty years earlier, North Korean government officials canceled the trip, claiming that poor weather made a search impossible. Tom returned home, vowing that he would try again.

THE VIETNAM WAR

The Struggle to Fight Communism in Southeast Asia

The war in Vietnam proved to be the most unpopular war in American history. It created deep and lasting divisions at home and caused thousands of casualties in a faraway country that most Americans, when the war began, couldn't place on a world map.

After World War II, with half of Germany and large parts of Eastern Europe under Communist control, the United States established a foreign policy dedicated to stopping Communist advances worldwide. One such place was Korea. Another was Vietnam, a former French colony that was in the throes of a civil war. Communists from the north, led by Ho Chi Minh, went to war against the anti-Communist south. Hanoi was the capital city of the north; Saigon was the capital of the south.

The United States feared that a Communist takeover of Vietnam would cause neighboring countries in Southeast Asia to fall to Communism, too. So in 1961, President John F. Kennedy sent in more than 3,000 American military advisers to help the South Vietnamese stop the Communists from taking over the entire country.

Military Buildup on Both Sides

The Saigon government suffered a series of defeats at the hands of a group of guerrilla fighters, the Viet Cong, who were backed by North Vietnam. So in 1964, President Lyndon Johnson decided to send large numbers of American ground troops to South Vietnam. Over the next few years, more and more soldiers were sent to Vietnam, with the number of troops peaking in early 1969 at 543,000. By this time, Hanoi was sending regular army units into South Vietnam, supplied with sophisticated weapons from their Russian and Chinese allies, to fight against U.S. forces.

At home, political and military leaders disagreed about the goals of the war. Officials in Washington believed that the purpose of the fighting

OPPOSITE: In 1967, helicopters of the U.S. 199th Light Infantry Brigade prepare to land near the Mekong Delta to pick up South Vietnamese rangers and transport them to another area of fighting.

was to keep the Communists from taking over in South Vietnam rather than defeating them in North Vietnam. To the military, this meant that victory would never be an option.

An Unpopular War

At first, most Americans supported the war. But that support faded as more soldiers were killed and wounded, while the White House could not offer a convincing reason for the sacrifices that American soldiers were making. At the war's worst point, about 200 American soldiers were being killed each week.

The American public began protesting against the war. By the late 1960s, large antiwar demonstrations became a common feature of American life, sometimes drawing hundreds of thousands of protesters who shut down cities across the country. The deep divisions caused by Vietnam made President Johnson so unpopular that he chose not to run for reelection in 1968. His successor, Richard Nixon, began a gradual withdrawal of U.S. forces in 1969, promising the South Vietnamese government support by air power rather than manpower.

By 1973, almost all of the American troops had been withdrawn. The South Vietnamese government was unable to hold off the North Vietnamese advance. The last American diplomatic personnel remaining in Saigon were forced to leave in April 1975; in a chaotic scene, they were evacuated

As the number of casualties grew and the war dragged on, an antiwar movement developed across America, with protesters holding massive demonstrations in cities all over the country. This button echoes the movement's basic demand: Bring the troops home.

A U.S. rocket team races toward a position to engage a Viet Cong squad in Vietnam, 1966. Rocket launchers—the weapon most commonly associated with U.S. troops in that conflict— were used extensively to smoke out the enemy from bunkers and trench-line positions.

from the American embassy and other locations, along with thousands of South Vietnamese officials and support staff (and their families) as Hanoi's army entered the city a few blocks away. The North Vietnamese overtook Saigon and renamed it Ho Chi Minh City.

The United States never lost a major battle in Vietnam, but in the end it lost the war. Nearly 60,000 Americans died there. The divisions caused by the war left scars on the American political system for decades and kept the heroism of the soldiers who fought in Vietnam from being acknowledged and appreciated.

A SOLDIER'S JOB

★ ★ ★ ★ ★

**"If I don't do my job, these guys
behind me ain't got a chance."**

Army sergeants have never been known to be easy on their soldiers. When artilleryman Sammy Davis was sent to Vietnam in 1967, he was assigned to a gun crew led by Sergeant Jim Gant. The sergeant demanded that the men pay attention to the smallest details, and Sammy thought Gant was hounding them out of sheer nastiness. "He was the meanest sergeant I'd ever seen," Sammy later recalled. "He'd make us take each bullet out of our clips every day and polish every one of them." Then twenty years old, he regarded the twenty-seven-year-old Gant as "a bitter old man." But as Sammy learned later in a desperate firefight, "Gant's meanness" had a purpose—and it may have saved his life.

★   ★   ★

Early in 1966, Sammy Davis's last year in high school, he was working at his part-time job at the local bowling alley in his hometown of Mooresville, Indiana, when a report on the television above the coffee counter caught his eye. It was a story about Roger Donlon, commander of a Special Forces team in Vietnam, who was the first man to receive the Medal of Honor in that war. Sammy looked at Donlon, ramrod straight as he received the medal from President Lyndon Johnson, and thought to himself, "I want to be a soldier like him." He enlisted in the Army right after graduation, volunteering for the artillery because his father had been an artilleryman in World War II. As soon as he finished his training, Sammy asked to be sent to Vietnam. He became part of Sergeant Gant's unit and reluctantly learned to pay attention to details.

On November 18, 1967, Sammy's battery unit of four guns and forty-two men was airlifted into an area on the Mekong Delta west of the city of Cai Lay. Its mission was to establish a forward fire support base named Cudgel to protect the American 9th Infantry Division operating in the area. Sammy's battery set up its 105mm howitzers near a canal.

Sammy Davis stands near his 105mm howitzer in Vietnam. This type of artillery, used in many operations in Vietnam, can fire various caliber shells at medium velocity and relatively high trajectory.

"Okay, Boys, Get Ready!"

As darkness fell, an officer arrived in a helicopter and told Sammy's unit, "Your possibility of getting hit tonight is 100 percent, so get ready." At 2:00 a.m., enemy mortars shelled the battery for half an hour. Then, after a moment of eerie calm, Sammy heard the shrill blare of whistles, along with shouts in broken English of "Go kill the GIs!" Sergeant Gant shouted, "Okay, boys, get ready!"

Sammy's crew inserted a "beehive" round into their howitzer—eight thousand one-inch-long steel darts designed to stop a huge enemy force like the one that appeared on the other side of the canal, some fifteen hundred men. When Gant gave the order, they fired. The North Vietnamese advanced, despite the rapid fire of the American artillery.

- BORN 1946, DAYTON, OHIO
- ENLISTED IN U.S. ARMY, 1966
- RANK: PRIVATE FIRST CLASS
- UNIT: BATTERY C, 2ND BATTALION, 4TH ARTILLERY, 9TH INFANTRY DIVISION
- SERVICE AT CAI LAY, SOUTH VIETNAM, 1967
- RECEIVED MEDAL OF HONOR, 1968

SAMMY DAVIS

A round from an enemy recoilless rifle hit the U.S. position, blowing Sammy into a trench. Before he lost consciousness, he saw that fragments from the round had hit Sergeant Gant in the chest.

When Sammy came to, he realized that the North Vietnamese were trying to take control of his howitzer and turn it around to fire on the Americans. Another 105mm gun positioned to the rear desperately fired a beehive round to stop them. Because of where he was lying, Sammy was hit in the back by several of the steel darts. He would have been killed if not for his flak jacket.

After watching several enemy troops run by him, Sammy stood up and grabbed his M16 rifle. "I had twelve clips," he says. "Which is roughly 180 rounds, and I started doing my job as a soldier. As I fired the last rounds, I didn't think that I was going to see daylight. But I wasn't going to quit because I thought, 'Well, if I don't do my job, these guys behind me ain't got a chance.'"

Sammy went back to the howitzer, determined to fire at least one round from the damaged artillery piece before being overrun. He managed to ram a shell into the gun and fired point-blank at the mass of North Vietnamese soldiers, who were advancing five deep directly in front of the gun.

At this point Sammy heard someone on the other side of the canal yell, "Don't shoot! I'm a GI." And he realized that American soldiers had been stranded there. "My God," he thought. "Somebody's got to go get them." Unable to swim because of the darts in his back and other injuries, he found an air mattress and used it to paddle across the canal during a lull in the action. He found three wounded soldiers, one of them suffering from a head wound that looked fatal. He got the gravely wounded man back across the canal, and then went back for the other two, floating them on the air mattress to the other side as well.

Finding Love in a Tough Old Sergeant

After rescuing the three Americans, Sammy was making his way back to a howitzer crew with a working gun so he could resume the fight when he saw Sergeant Gant lying on the ground, badly wounded, his body halfway in the water. Gant held up his hand; Sammy crawled up and grabbed it as "that light bulb your daddy always told you about came on." In that moment, he realized that all the drills and details his sergeant had made him and the others go through hadn't been intended to punish them, but to help them survive. "I looked down in his eyes and knew that he didn't hate me. He loved me."

As the battle subsided, Sammy counted eleven other men out of the original forty-two in his unit who were still standing. The man with

At the battle of Khe Sanh in May 1967, marines heroically held off a large force of North Vietnamese troops. This recoilless rifle was aimed at an enemy position about 1,000 yards away. Viet Cong strategy sometimes involved encroaching on American positions and attempting to seize guns and artillery to use against U.S. troops.

the gaping head wound he had brought back from the other side of the canal—it was Jim Deister, but Sammy didn't yet know his name—had been placed with the dead. (See pages 87–93 for Jim's story.) But a medic passing by realized that the soldier was still breathing and quickly readied him to be evacuated by helicopter to a field hospital.

"I didn't do anything heroic," Sammy said after being awarded the Medal of Honor. "I did my job. That's what soldiers do. And if there was one of these given for that night, there should be at least forty-two of them given. The reason we fought so hard was because we discovered that we loved each other, that we were all we had. And we became brothers. And those men that I fought with are still my brothers. I went to war, and when I got over there I learned about what real love is."

Sammy Davis receives the Medal of Honor from President Lyndon Johnson in 1968. Footage of his award ceremony was used in the 1994 film *Forrest Gump*, with actor Tom Hanks's head superimposed over Davis's.

Private Deister was one of the first and most grievously wounded soldiers rescued by Sammy Davis in 1967. He didn't find out who saved his life for another two decades, when he happened to come across the story in a book about the Medal of Honor.

A Life Saved

BY JIM DEISTER

In the fall of 1967, I was a twenty-one-year-old army private in the 3rd Platoon of C Company, 15th Engineer Battalion, operating in the upper Mekong Delta of South Vietnam. As a combat engineer I was responsible for constructing firing positions, placing and detonating explosives, removing obstacles, and detecting mines.

I had left behind a wife and daughter, Jamie, who was born just nineteen days before I started my tour in Vietnam. I held her in my arms only for a short while during a brief leave before deploying.

On November 16, 1967, my twenty-second birthday, our unit was ordered to go by helicopter into an area west of Cai Lay, South Vietnam, near the Cambodian border, where there had been a large buildup in enemy forces. As we approached the landing area, the door gunners on our helicopter were blazing away. We landed and scrambled out of the chopper, moving quickly to a nearby dike. We hunkered down and began to trade fire with a group of Viet Cong moving toward us. An hour or so later, artillery and gunships were called in to suppress the enemy gunfire, allowing

Jim Deister was twenty-one when he left behind his wife and newborn daughter, Jamie, and shipped out for Vietnam in 1967.

us to move up to a tree line, where we kicked some pigs out of the area and made camp. It was a memorable way to spend a birthday—pinned down for the night in what was basically a pig sty, slapping at mosquitos, picking leeches off our legs and arms, and being pretty scared.

The following morning, we loaded up with a reconnaissance platoon and headed to a remote support base named Cudgel to support an infantry company operating in that area. When we got there, our demolition team was directed to set up its position across a large canal while most of the infantry remained on the other side. Sandbags had been flown in; we filled them up and laid them around holes in the ground to make "bunkers" because we had been told that the enemy would certainly mortar us and possibly launch an assault.

When we first crossed the canal to establish our position—pushing our weapons, packs, and other supplies over the water on air mattresses— I noticed an artillery piece, a 105mm howitzer, sitting near a depression in the ground. At the time, I had no idea that one of the artillerymen operating it would soon save my life.

At about 2:00 a.m., we heard a mortar slide down a tube, a sound that you never forget. The explosion was close. More mortars rained down, and then the enemy began its assault, yelling, in almost perfect English, "You die tonight, GI! We kill you tonight, GI!"

Shadowy forms emerged from the darkness, wearing pith helmets and backpacks and carrying AK-47 rifles. These were disciplined North Vietnamese soldiers, not the Viet Cong guerrillas we were used to engaging.

Suddenly, something hit me and knocked me down. My records say it was a gunshot wound to the chest. I was also hit in the head. As I lay on the trail, trying to catch my breath, North Vietnamese soldiers kept running by me toward the canal. A fellow soldier who didn't know me, Gwendell Holloway, saw me lying on the trail and came out of cover to drag me to a hole on the edge of the canal where there was a third soldier.

At this point, things got hazy for me. As I tried to focus, the rest of the battle became a sort of slide show, where you see a slide, then miss two or three, then see another. Much of what was happening didn't make sense. But one thing was clear: the face of a red-haired guy coming to rescue me. Then I was on my back floating in the middle of the canal, watching the flares lighting up the place like daylight and thinking, "Turn off the damn lights! They'll see us!"

The next thing I remember, I was in a hospital, and people were holding me down while I tried to get back to the battle and my buddies. I remember clearly a nice-looking nurse smiling as she handed me a note that said, "Do you know where you are?" I replied, "Last night I was in the Mekong Delta." She wrote me another note that said, "That was three weeks ago, and you are in Japan. They will be taking you home to the United States soon." Sure enough, on December 24, 1967, I arrived at Fitzsimons Army Medical Center in Denver. My wife, my parents, and my little daughter, Jamie, were there to meet me.

More bits and pieces of that night eventually came together, but I never found out exactly how I survived and whether I was the only one in my unit to have gotten back to safety across the canal. During my hospitalization, the staff gave my father my medical records. I was shocked at what they said: "PFC Deister was initially seen at the 3rd Evac Hospital with a six-inch circumference wound on the right side of his head, with brain matter protruding from the wound. A 9mm bullet was removed from his midbrain. He had multiple fragment and gunshot wounds to the lower chest and right elbow."

On October 1, 1968, after a ten-month stay in the hospital and intense rehabilitation, I was retired from the Army because of a physical disability. I returned to my hometown, Ulysses, Kansas, and went to work for a rural electric company as an apprentice lineman. Soon, I decided I needed to go back to school and find another occupation.

I completed bachelor's and master's degrees in psychology at Emporia State University in Kansas. I did my internship as a rehabilitation counselor at the Veterans Administration Center in Wichita, Kansas, then moved my family to Salina, Kansas, where I started a job as a rehabilitation counselor and got on with my life.

Could I have been that man with the head wound on the other side of the canal whom Sammy carried to safety?

More than fifteen years later, in 1988, I was browsing in a bookstore when I noticed a book describing the actions of Medal of Honor recipients in Vietnam. I opened the book, and a date, November 18, 1967, caught my eye. The place—"near Cai Lay, South Vietnam"—really grabbed my attention. I began to read the story of Sammy L. Davis and the actions that had earned him the Medal of Honor on that date and in that place.

When I got to the point in the story where Sammy found three Americans, one of them shot in the head, my heart came up into my throat. Could I have been that man with the head wound on the other side of the canal whom Sammy carried to safety? My hands were shaking as I took the book to the counter and paid for it. I read that story again and again, and what was described was very close to the bits that I remembered. I had to get in touch with this Sammy Davis!

A few weeks later, the Vietnam Traveling Memorial Wall—a replica of the Vietnam Veterans Memorial in Washington, DC—came to Salina. When I asked one of the sponsors if he knew Sammy Davis, his eyes grew wide. "He's a friend of mine, and he's looking for *you*!" he replied.

The next morning, Sammy called my office and asked me some detailed questions about where I was when I was wounded. The answers convinced him that I was the soldier he had rescued. We arranged to meet a few weeks later, at the hotel where the Nebraska Vietnam Veterans Reunion was being held. It was there that I saw a familiar face enter the lobby. Chills went up my spine: It was the same red-haired soldier I'd seen the night I'd been wounded! Sammy walked right up to me and gave me a big hug. "I've seen you before," he said.

Sammy told me how his crew had lowered the angle of the artillery pieces to fire the beehive rounds because they thought everyone across the canal had been killed and they had to stop the attack they were facing. My buddy Gwendell Holloway felt something had to be done, so he jumped up and started waving his bush hat and yelling, "Help us! We are GIs." Sammy came across the canal to rescue him. That's when he found out there were actually three wounded soldiers trapped on the other side.

Sammy's initial feeling that night was that I was dead since he couldn't feel a pulse, but he didn't want to leave my body, so he threw

GIs fought under extremely difficult conditions in South Vietnam, including dense jungle terrain. Moving the wounded in these swamps was especially difficult and dangerous work.

me over his shoulders in a fireman's carry and took me back to the canal. The other guys he also rescued were holding on to his arms, and every so often he would have to lay me down and shield them while he fought off the enemy all around us. When we got to the crossing, he put me on an air mattress faceup because he didn't want my head to drop into the water, and started across. He let an infantry officer and an artilleryman who met him in the water take me to the other side, then went back to get the other two wounded Americans, including Gwendell, and bring them to safety.

That conversation with Sammy in North Platte, Nebraska, was the beginning of a lifelong friendship. Like most people, I've always wondered why these men do such remarkable things. What makes them perform gallant acts above and beyond the normal call of duty to save

Jim Deister (right) had been badly wounded and would have died if a fellow soldier—one he didn't know—hadn't risked his own life to rescue him. More than twenty years later, Jim learned the name of his savior: Medal of Honor recipient Sammy Davis (left).

others? After years of knowing Sammy, I think I have some answers. He is simply a good man, raised to do the right things, and the right thing on that bloody night of November 18, 1967, was taking care of a man he didn't know by name but knew in his heart to be his brother.

> "You must be willing to live for your country."

It's amazing to listen to Sammy talk about his experiences. He tells veterans to be proud of their service, something they may not have heard from others because the scars of that unpopular war are still with us. He lets schoolchildren pass his Medal of Honor around and explains its importance, always emphasizing that it is not *won* but is *received* for having performed one's duty.

Once, when I was having terrible guilt feelings about having lived when so many others died, Sam invited me to go with him to the tenth anniversary of the Vietnam Veterans Memorial in Washington, DC. I stood with him at the top of the memorial as he gave a speech I had heard him give before. "You not only must be willing to die for your country, you must also be willing to live for your country!" he said. I thought, "That's me. I need to live as well as I can, and continue to serve my country." That became a sort of motto for my life. I became more involved in veterans' organizations, and with another veteran I started a support group working with Vietnam veterans and their spouses. It helped me as well as them deal with our past.

Sam is a Vietnam brother for sure, but he is more than that; he is a part of my family. When my parents were still alive, they thought of him as another son. My children and grandchildren, including my youngest grandson, who bears my name, know that they are alive because of him. We all remember the man who risked his life to save me and two others on a very dark night in 1967 and kept another name from appearing on the Vietnam wall along with the tens of thousands of those who gave their all.

TEN MINUTES
OF HELL

**"I have to take care of the injured.
They'd do it for me."**

Alfred Rascon was only four years old when his parents left their home in Chihuahua, Mexico, in 1947 for the United States. They settled in the California town of Oxnard. Afraid of not being able to stay in the country, they never applied to become citizens. Referred to as "Alfredo" on official school forms, Alfred was aware that he was different from his classmates, but he always knew where he belonged. "I am Mexican by birth," he likes to say, "and American by choice."

An only child, Alfred was fascinated by the servicemen he saw leaving for the Korean War from the nearby naval station at Port Hueneme. He fantasized about being one of them, even making parachutes out of old sheets and staging imaginary combat jumps off the roof of his house.

The desire to give something back to the country that had accepted him and his family prompted him to join the Army soon after graduating from high school in 1963. By 1965, he was in Vietnam serving as a medic in a reconnaissance platoon. The men in his unit called him Doc and counted on him to be there when they needed him. He never disappointed them.

In the spring of 1966, Alfred's battalion was part of a major operation in the jungles near Long Khanh Province. The Americans had been facing growing resistance from small units of North Vietnamese troops for a few days and finding large caches of weapons and supplies. Alfred had a sinking feeling that the enemy was preparing to launch a large offensive.

On March 16, Alfred's platoon was on a morning patrol when the calm was shattered by sounds of a major battle less than a mile away. Another U.S. battalion was surrounded and under a severe attack by a large enemy force. Alfred's unit moved out immediately to help. They were walking single file along a narrow jungle trail when North Vietnamese fighters hidden in the undergrowth ahead suddenly opened fire. It was the beginning of what Alfred would later call his "ten minutes of hell."

As a medic, "Doc" Rascon carried a backpack filled with supplies that often weighed more than 30 pounds and had the choice of carrying a pistol or M16 rifle.

The Nightmare Begins

The soldier at the head of the column was struck by several bullets and fell to the ground. The rest of the platoon dived for cover and hugged the ground as heavy fire whizzed over their heads. "It was as if the earth was about to break up," Alfred recalled. "It was total chaos. I had no idea what was going on in front of me other than the fact that somebody said, 'Hey, Doc, somebody's wounded.'"

Alfred's platoon sergeant screamed at him to stay put. "I said okay, and then took off and went forward anyway," Alfred remembers. Three

· BORN 1945, CHIHUAHUA, MEXICO
· ENLISTED IN U.S. ARMY, 1963
· RANK: SPECIALIST FOURTH CLASS
· UNIT: 1ST BATTALION (AIRBORNE), 503RD
  INFANTRY, 173RD AIRBORNE BRIGADE
  (SEPARATE)
· SERVICE IN LONG KHANH PROVINCE,
  VIETNAM
· RECEIVED MEDAL OF HONOR, 2000

ED RASCON

times he tried to reach his fallen buddy, but each time he got stopped by the heavy gunfire. "I don't know what possessed me to try again, but I got up and got to him." He shielded the soldier from enemy fire with his own body for a moment, then began to drag him to safety. Moving backward, he was hit in the hip by a bullet that traveled upward through his body alongside his spine and exited at his collarbone. He managed to pull his buddy to a protected spot, but the soldier was already dead.

Alfred heard one of his comrades, whose machine-gun fire was preventing the North Vietnamese from overrunning the platoon yelling, "Ammo! Ammo! I need ammo!" Alfred stripped two bandoliers of 7.62 caliber shells off the dead soldier's body and despite his wounds ran forward with them as bullets buzzed around him. When he reached the machine gunner, he saw that the soldier was wounded and treated him as best he could.

Moments later, a grenade exploded near Alfred's head. Feeling blood streaming down his cheek, he thought to himself, "Oh, my God, my face is gone." He reassured himself by running his fingers over his nose and forehead. "For a moment I didn't want to take care of anyone anymore, but I had to come back and put myself together again and regain my composure," he remembered. "I told myself, 'I have to go out and take care of the injured; they'd do it for me.'"

When another grenade landed near one of his buddies, Alfred dived on top of him and took the impact with his own body. The explosion blew Alfred's helmet off his head and the backpack off his body.

By now Alfred was no longer able to walk. He crawled from one wounded GI to another as the fighting continued to rage all around him. He was bleeding from his ears, mouth, and nose, but he refused morphine because he feared it would keep him from thinking clearly enough to take care of his comrades.

Receiving Last Rites

Fighting to remain conscious, Alfred was finally taken to a field hospital. Doctors there thought he might not make it, and a Catholic chaplain was called to give him last rites. But Alfred survived a long operation.

As soon as he was strong enough to travel, Alfred was sent to a hospital in Japan, where he spent nearly five months recuperating. He heard that he had been recommended for the Medal of Honor, but nothing happened, and he forgot about it. He just wanted to go back to school and get on with his life.

After being discharged from active duty in 1966, Alfred joined the U.S. Army Reserves, went to college, and finally became a naturalized citizen. In 1969, he returned to active duty, graduated from Officer Candidate School as a second lieutenant, and went back to Vietnam for a second tour. He remained in the Army until his retirement in 1984.

Alfred endured "ten minutes of hell" in a 1966 firefight in which he saved the lives of several comrades and kept his platoon from being destroyed. Badly wounded himself, he was helped back to safety by two other GIs.

Correcting History

At a 1993 reunion of his original platoon, the men whose lives Alfred had saved during those ten minutes of hell in 1966 learned that he had never received the Medal of Honor. Without his knowledge, they asked

(Alfred's story continues on page 100.)

MEDICS: *Treating the Wounded on the Battlefield*

A medic gives an injured buddy a drink of water. Searing heat and tropical conditions in the Vietnam War made fresh, clean water a vital commodity for wounded soldiers.

In combat, where everyone else is trying to take lives, the medic's job is to save them. He is often exposed to hostile fire as he rushes to the aid of the wounded. And he is often among the first casualties in a firefight.

Originally, the medic often wore a red cross armband on the battlefield and wasn't targeted by the enemy. But during World War II, the enemy realized that one medic could often patch up several wounded soldiers well enough to let them go on fighting, so it made sense to try to take him out. Especially during the Pacific War against Japan, the red cross symbol became a bull's-eye for enemy snipers. U.S. Army medics and Navy corpsmen began to carry arms, often a pistol, to protect themselves and the men they treated on the battlefield.

Essential Tools and Supplies

The backpack ("aid bag") that today's medic carries weighs about thirty pounds. What it contains depends to some degree on how long the mission is and the environment in which it takes place. Generally, it includes such tools as tourniquets, splints, trauma scissors, helmet-mounted flashlights for night missions, and tubing to administer intravenous saline solutions and blood plasma. Of special importance are Emergency Trauma Dressing and special gauze to stop hemorrhages, because severe blood loss is responsible for roughly half of all battlefield deaths. The aid bag also typically contains seals to treat sucking chest wounds caused by bullets or shrapnel tearing into the lungs, and devices to keep airways open, including scalpels to perform emergency tracheotomies.

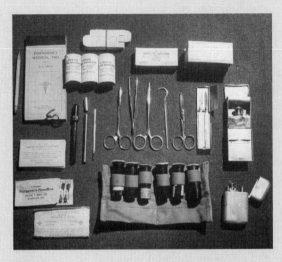

A selection of surgical tools carried by the Army Medical Corps personnel during World War II. The lighter (lower right corner) was used to sterilize instruments to prevent infection during lifesaving procedures on the battlefield.

Medics carry a variety of drugs ranging from over-the-counter remedies such as aspirin, stomach antacids, and salve for athlete's foot to heavy-duty medicines such as morphine for severe pain, antibiotics for infection, and epinephrine to counteract serious allergic reactions.

One prescription medics give all soldiers in the field: Drink lots of water!

the Army what had happened. His medal recommendation had gotten lost in red tape, they were told. They asked the Defense Department to reopen the files and enlisted the help of their congressmen. When one official accused them of wanting to change history, Alfred's former platoon sergeant said, "No, we don't want to change history. We just want to correct it."

Some of the men Alfred had served with were with him at the White House ceremony when he was awarded the medal. Alfred asked them to stand and said that the medal was not just for him, but for all of them. Afterward, Neil Haffey, one of the men whose body Alfred had protected with his own from an exploding grenade, reminded the audience that while bravery is an individual choice, it's also a choice that has consequences for others. "I have a beautiful wife," Haffey said. "I have four children and four grandchildren. I wouldn't have any of that without Doc. I would be dead." Later that day, Alfred and his friends went to the Vietnam Veterans Memorial and stood silently in front of the names of the men from their platoon who had died that day in 1966 near Long Khanh Province.

For his acts of bravery as a medic in the jungles of Vietnam, Alfred was awarded the Medal of Honor in 2000 by President Bill Clinton. His recommendation had gotten lost in red tape for thirty-four years.

After America was attacked on 9/11, Alfred, now fifty-six years old, rejoined the Army Reserves as a major in the Medical Service Corps. He served in Afghanistan and Iraq and retired for good in 2006.

MAXIMUM RESISTANCE

> **"I believed that the most important thing
> in my life was to return from North Vietnam
> with honor, not just to return."**

Bud Day answered his nation's call three times, in three wars. He began his combat career in World War II, as an eighteen-year-old private in the Pacific. In 1950, as an air national guardsman and fighter pilot, he was ordered to Korea, the first war in which jet planes played a major role. By 1967, he was a part of the military elite, an air force major flying dangerous missions over North Vietnam—a rank that would also mean he would face brutal treatment if his jet was shot down and he were captured. But as he had shown through his entire life, Bud could outlast just about anyone or anything thrown at him—and in a North Vietnamese prison, that's exactly what he had to do.

George Day, known as "Bud" from the time he was a boy, was a seventeen-year-old high school junior in Sioux City, Iowa, when the Japanese attacked Pearl Harbor, Hawaii, and America went to war. A few months later, he was glued to the radio, along with most Americans, listening to reports of Lieutenant Colonel Jimmy Doolittle's daring air raid on Tokyo, Japan. Doolittle had led a group of B-25 bombers taking off from the aircraft carrier USS *Hornet* in a surprise attack against the Japanese

- BORN 1925, SIOUX CITY, IOWA
- FIRST ENLISTED AS VOLUNTEER FOR MARINES, 1942, AT AGE 17
- RANK: MAJOR, U.S. AIR FORCE
- SERVICE AS POW IN HANOI, NORTH VIETNAM, 1967-73
- PREVIOUSLY SERVED IN WWII AND KOREA
- RECEIVED MEDAL OF HONOR, 1976
- DIED, 2013

BUD DAY

mainland. It was a risky move—bombers had never flown from an aircraft carrier before—but it paid off. The U.S. strike showed Japan's warlords that their country would have to pay for having started the war, and it gave Americans back home the hope that the United States was able to fight back. (For more on Doolittle's raid, see the essay "My Grandfather the War Hero," on pages 14–19.)

Doolittle, who was awarded a Medal of Honor for this action, became one of Bud's heroes and made him want to be a flyer himself someday. But first Bud just wanted to get into the war. He was tough and stubborn, and despite his family's objections, he dropped out of school not long after the Doolittle raid to join the Marines. He spent nearly three years in the Pacific serving with a 130mm gun battery, and then came home to get his high school diploma, graduate from college, and get a law degree. He began work as an attorney in 1949, but because he felt that the peace that followed World War II wouldn't last, he joined the Iowa Air National Guard to fulfill his boyhood dream of becoming an aviator and to be ready if trouble came.

Bud joined the Air National Guard in 1950, then a year later was called to active duty as a fighter pilot during the Korean War. He served two tours flying the F-84 Thunderjet, the Air Force's primary strike aircraft during the war. Promoted to captain, he decided to make the Air Force his career.

Flying over Vietnam

In 1967, Bud, who had by then reached the rank of major, decided to volunteer for Vietnam even though he was less than a year away from retirement. Within weeks he was leading a detachment of F-100 Super Sabre jets whose top secret mission was to act as forward air controllers for U.S. fighter-bombers operating over North Vietnam and Laos. It was a dangerous job because the F-100s had to direct air strikes by these fighter-bombers while continuing to circle over the target so that they could check on how effective these strikes had been. "It was a really hairy mission because you spent a lot of time fairly low to the ground getting shot at," Bud later said. "I lost almost half of my airplanes in the first six months we operated."

In 1967, Bud Day was assigned to lead a fleet of Super Sabre fighter-bombers in attacks over North Vietnam and Laos. Sixty-five missions later, he was shot down over North Vietnam.

On August 26, Bud, who by then had logged sixty-five missions, was in the air over North Vietnam directing a group of U.S. fighter-bombers in an attack against an enemy surface-to-air missile site. Suddenly, he felt his plane lurch. It had been hit by antiaircraft fire and was soon spiraling out of control. Bud ejected, but as he did, he smashed into the cockpit, breaking his arm in three places and injuring his back. North Vietnamese militiamen below watched his parachute open and were waiting for him when he landed.

Bud knew that he had just entered a situation where he had only two choices—to submit or resist.

The militiamen marched him a few miles to an underground shelter and began to interrogate him violently. When he refused to answer their questions, they pretended they were going to execute him by aiming a pistol at his head and pulling the trigger. Bud tensed for the explosion, but there was only the click of the firing pin hitting an empty chamber, followed by his captors' laughter. Then they used a rope to suspend him upside down from a rafter by his feet. After several hours, believing him to be so badly hurt from his shattered arm and damaged back that he wouldn't try to escape, they let him down, tied him up, and left him in a corner of the shelter.

The Great Escape

Four days later, as a pair of distracted teenaged soldiers stood guard outside, Bud managed to untie the rope and escape out of the back of the shelter. He headed south—"toward freedom," as he said. At first he was slogging through rice paddies. Then the terrain turned to light forest and he was able to make better time. When darkness fell on his second night on the run, Bud, by then feverish from his wounds, crawled into some undergrowth to get some sleep, not realizing that he was next to a North Vietnamese artillery position.

The F-100 Super Sabre jet was long and sleek, with low-set wings and tail. It was the first U.S. Air Force fighter capable of supersonic speed in level flight.

When the big guns began to fire the next morning, the boom of the shells left Bud bleeding from his ears and nose. He collected himself and continued to hobble south, successfully evading the enemy patrols chasing him. He lived on berries and frogs he trapped along the way. Floating on a bamboo log, he crossed a river and passed through the "demilitarized zone" that divided North and South Vietnam.

Sometime between the twelfth and fifteenth day after his escape— by then Bud was hallucinating as a result of pain and hunger and had lost track of time—he heard helicopters and stumbled toward the sound. In the distance, he saw a clearing in the jungle where U.S. choppers were evacuating a marine unit. He limped toward the landing zone, calling out to the Americans. But his voice was drowned out by the noise of the rotors throttled for takeoff, and the helicopters left before he could get close enough to get their attention.

The next morning, heading south again, Bud was spotted by the North Vietnamese who had been on his trail for two weeks. Delirious, he mumbled to himself, "I didn't come this far to surrender," and took off running. The enemy patrol shot him in the hand and leg. He was recaptured within a mile of a U.S. Marine firebase and taken back to the camp from which he had escaped. There he was tortured again. His right arm, which had begun to heal, was rebroken.

Staying Alive

Over the next several days, Bud was shuttled from one enemy camp to another. Finally, he arrived at the Hanoi Hilton, as American prisoners of war there had sarcastically named the squalid prison complex on the outskirts of North Vietnam's capital city. (Read more about the Hanoi Hilton on pages 108–9.)

Bud's untreated wounds were infected, he was suffering from malnutrition, and he was unable to perform the simplest tasks for himself. His cell mate, another American flyer named Norris Overly, put a

Bud Day had already served in two wars when he went to Vietnam in 1967. He retired from the military ten years later, one of the most highly decorated officers in U.S. military history.

splint on his arm and helped him survive over the next few weeks.

Not long after Bud was put in prison, another downed pilot, John McCain, a future U.S. senator and presidential candidate, was brought to their cell after having been in solitary confinement for several weeks. Unable to feed or clean himself, McCain was near death. But, he later said, "Bud and Norris wouldn't let me die. They bathed me, fed me, nursed me, encouraged me, and ordered me back to life. They saved my life, but more than that, Bud showed me how to save my self-respect and my honor."

There were several hundred American prisoners of war at the Hanoi Hilton, almost all of them pilots who had been shot down and captured. They were forced to endure brutal torture—beaten with sticks, suspended from the ceilings of their cells by ropes until their arms tore loose from their shoulder sockets, locked into iron shackles on their wood-plank beds for days at a time. "It was just absolute filth," Bud later recalled. "You had rats running around. And we were on about seven hundred calories a day of food. So you're all emaciated with big, sunken eyes, and your health was in great danger."

The Americans survived by staying disciplined and keeping their command structure inside the prison—by remaining servicemen instead of becoming prisoners. The North Vietnamese tried to prevent this sense of discipline and organization by separating the POWs and placing them in isolated cells, but the prisoners developed a "tap code" that allowed them to "talk" by tapping the walls of their cells with their knuckles.

Bud became one of the leaders the rest of the POWs looked to as an example. Because of his "bad attitude," in the words of one of the commanders of the Hanoi Hilton—when tortured, he gave false information; when given orders, he disobeyed—Bud was subjected to even more sadistic treatment than the other Americans. Once, he was strapped down on a table and beaten with an automobile fan belt. He tried to divert himself from thinking about the pain by counting the strokes hitting his body. When he reached three hundred, he said to himself, "Why am I wasting my time counting? They're going to kill me." He drifted in and out of consciousness as the beating continued.

> **The prisoners developed a "tap code" that allowed them to "talk" by tapping the walls of their cells with their knuckles.**

Never Giving In

Always defying those who had the power of life and death over him, Bud spent the next five years trying to show the other POWs that they were still free Americans despite being imprisoned and helping them survive captivity. He earned a reputation for giving his North Vietnamese tormenters only one thing—"maximum resistance." When he was asked later how he kept from giving in, he said, "I believed that the most important thing in my life was to return from North Vietnam with honor, not just to return."

One incident that the prisoners never forgot occurred in 1971, when a group of them were trying to hold a forbidden religious service. North Vietnamese guards entered the room they were in, pointing rifles at them. Bud moved so close to them that he was looking directly down the barrels of the guns. Then he began to loudly sing "The Star-Spangled Banner." The other prisoners joined him. The North Vietnamese guards looked around nervously, not sure what to do next. Eventually, the Americans were allowed to continue their prayer service.

(Bud's story continues on page 110.)

AMERICAN POWS:
Resistance and Survival

Most of the American POWs resisted their North Vietnamese captors in some way. Two of them in the prison known as the Hanoi Hilton, along with Bud Day, were especially heroic, according to the stories told by other prisoners.

Jeremiah Denton (shown in the film strip at right) was forced by prison guards to be interviewed by a foreign journalist for a propaganda film. He was supposed to denounce the war in Vietnam and say that American servicemen were war criminals. Instead, he shambled into the interview room with a grim look on his face, stared up at the bright camera lights, and began blinking his eyes in a deliberate way. The guards didn't understand what he was doing, but American officials who later saw the film realized Denton was spelling out T-O-R-T-U-R-E in the dots and dashes of Morse code with his eye blinks. It was the first information they had received about what the POWs were facing. Denton was tortured again after the filming because of what he said to the interviewer: "Whatever the position of my government is, I support it fully . . . and I will as long as I live."

U.S. Navy Commander Jeremiah Denton was filmed in a televised propaganda interview in 1966. He alerted Americans to what was taking place in the notorious Hanoi Hilton prison by blinking T-O-R-T-U-R-E in Morse code.

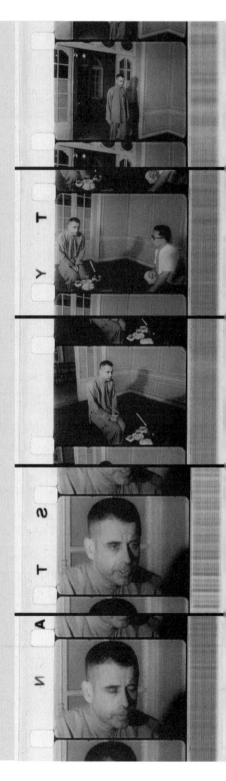

Extreme Measures

James Stockdale, the senior naval officer in the prison, also helped create a spirit of defiance among the other POWs. Once, when he was about to be paraded before foreign newsmen, he slit his scalp with a rusty razor blade he had hidden in his cell so that observers wouldn't think the prisoners were being treated well. When the guards put a hat on his bloody wounds and tried to continue the propaganda stunt, he picked up a stool and used it to bash his face until it was disfigured almost beyond recognition. Later, when he was about to be tortured into giving up the names of other POWs who were resisting, he used his razor blade again, this time to slit his wrists so that he wouldn't betray anyone. Prison doctors kept him alive. From that moment,

North Vietnamese authorities, seeing that the Americans were ready to die rather than be dishonored, moderated the use of torture against them.

Jeremiah Denton and James Stockdale returned home after the POWs were finally released in 1973 and resumed their naval careers, both retiring as admirals. Stockdale was awarded the Medal of Honor in 1976 and was the running mate of Ross Perot when he ran for president of the United States. Denton was elected to the U.S. Senate from his home state of Alabama in 1980 and served until 1986.

American prisoners stand at attention in their jail cell at the Hanoi Hilton just before they are released, 1973.

Bud was released with the other POWs on March 14, 1973, following negotiations between North Vietnam and the United States. Three years later, President Gerald Ford presented him with the Medal of Honor. The citation read, in part: "His conduct in the face of lethal enemy pressure was a lifesaving inspiration to his fellow inmates."

Bud was one of America's most highly decorated servicemen and a hero to others in his later years, just as Jimmy Doolittle had been to him when he was a boy. He was also one of the most outspoken on the subject of patriotism. "We've been fortunate by an accident of birth to be born Americans," he often said in the interviews he gave until his death in 2013. "And having had that good fortune, our primary duty is to make sure that this country survives and that we stay free. That ought to be the primary objective of every American every day for the rest of their lives."

At his retirement from the military in 1977, Bud Day (second from right) stands with President Gerald Ford (left) and fellow Medal of Honor recipients James Stockdale (second from left) and Tommy Norris (right). For Tommy's story, see pages 117–27.

★ ★ ★ ★ ★ ★ ★ ★ ★

Shot down over North Vietnam in 1967, Major Thorsness spent
the next six years in the notorious Hanoi Hilton prison camp,
with 600 other U.S. aviators. What saved him was communicating
with his fellow prisoners and the power of prayer. He received
the Medal of Honor in 1973.

★ ★ ★ ★ ★ ★ ★ ★ ★

Surviving Hell

BY LEO K. THORSNESS

On April 19, 1967, I was flying my F-105 "Wild Weasel" fighter jet over North Vietnam—my ninety-third mission—when I saw that the plane on my wing had been hit by enemy 85mm flak and was going down. The pilot and his backseater bailed out. As their parachutes opened, an enemy fighter jet rolled in to machine-gun them in the air. I shot it down before it could kill the defenseless men. Because we were low on fuel, we hightailed it to an air-refueling tanker, then returned to the action to help direct a possible rescue of the guys who had bailed out and were now on the ground. During the air fight that followed, we damaged another enemy fighter and chased off two more before our fuel gauges showed near empty, forcing us to climb to thirty-five thousand feet and then glide more than eighty miles to a Thailand recovery base. I would receive the Medal of Honor for this mission, although I didn't find out about the award until years later.

 This was because about two weeks later, my own plane was hit by an enemy air-to-air missile over North Vietnam, and my backseater, Harry

Johnson, and I had to bail out. As I floated earthward, I tried to assess what I knew was serious damage to my back and knees when I ejected from the plane at seven hundred miles an hour. I realized that I had gone in an instant from a high-tech heavily armed aircraft to a no-tech parachute and a place where I would be captured by men with machetes.

I would spend the next six years with several hundred downed aviators as a prisoner of war (POW) in a prison we called the Hanoi Hilton. My time as a POW was divided into two more or less equal periods. The first three years were brutal, characterized by excruciating torture, totally inadequate food—normally green-weed soup and dirty rice—and long periods of solitary confinement. The last three years were more bearable by comparison. We lived in larger cells of fifteen to forty-five prisoners and were able to talk out loud, eat a little more food (including bread made with weevil-infested flour), and endure fewer brutal beatings for breaking even minor prison rules.

> I had gone in an instant from a high-tech heavily armed aircraft to a no-tech parachute and a place where I would be captured by men with machetes.

Upon arrival in Hanoi, interrogation began immediately in a small torture room. I was suspended from a hook on the ceiling, hanging by my arms during torture. A sinister collection of paraphernalia was piled in the corner (ropes, nylon straps, two metal U-bolts, and a long metal rod). The interrogators used this equipment to make me and my fellow POWs talk.

Between interrogations, I was kept in a small room roughly six by seven feet with a cement slab and old-fashioned stocks, and no toilet facilities. I was bound by my ankles and wrists for days at a time. To get through the pain, I broke time into short blocks, telling myself, "Leo, hold out another one minute . . . another thirty seconds . . ."

But after eighteen days and nights of torture following my arrival at the prison, time became blurred and without structure. After even

Leo Thorsness climbs into the cockpit of his F-105 "Wild Weasel" fighter-bomber (1967), equipped with radar-seeking missiles used to destroy the radars and surface-to-air missile installations of enemy air defense systems.

more days and nights of torture sessions—I can't remember how many—I broke. I went beyond the Geneva Convention POW requirements of giving only name, rank, serial number, and date of birth. That devastated me—I felt there must be others who had endured the same horrific torture and emerged with their honor intact. It was only after I was moved to a cell with another badly injured POW and shared my experience that I was told, to my great relief, "Leo, everyone who goes through that kind of torture—either they break or they die. Some did both."

For a time I lived in solitary confinement or with one or two other POWs in a small cell. Any sound we made or protest against the brutal conditions brought an instant beating, or we were made to kneel on rough concrete for hours. Agonizing torture was as routine as the festering untreated wounds and malnutrition we all suffered from.

I was not the strongest or weakest of the prisoners. I was an average guy there, just as I had been in my life before I was shot down and captured.

How did I survive this hell? First, like all the other prisoners, I knew that while my captors were trying literally to keep me in the dark, I wasn't alone. We prisoners communicated by tapping on the walls of the Hanoi Hilton in defiance of our captors' efforts to keep us isolated and helpless. (That's how I found out I had been chosen to receive the Medal of Honor.) Second, I prayed and prayed: for my freedom, for other prisoners, especially those being tortured, and mostly for my wife and daughter. Our captors owned everything about us except our minds.

Our effort to take control of our lives was comprised of a lot of imagination. One day, for instance, as a guard took three of us to a walled cistern for a sponge bath, we spotted a piece of a 35mm filmstrip and snuck it back to our cell. We converted millimeters into inches and put a small stitch at each inch in the drawstring of one of our prison pajamas—using it as a tape measure to determine the distance we could cover by walking along the edges of our cell: exactly twenty-five feet. Two hundred twenty-five laps would be a mile. We calculated that in ten hours we would walk ten miles (we changed direction each twenty-five laps to avoid dizziness). It was ten thousand miles from Hanoi back to the United States, where my wife and daughter were. I became convinced that if I walked ten hours a day, six days a week, I'd be "home" with them in 3.2 years! I was overjoyed each day I walked ten miles. I was walking toward freedom.

> Our captors owned everything about us except our minds.

Another time, I found a rusty nail and spent days drilling a peep hole in the mortar so I could watch other POWs walking by in the inner courtyard, and especially the guards standing there. As an especially brutal guard walked by one day, I imagined myself flipping an imaginary dime. I caught it as it came down and slapped it on the back of my

Shot down over North Vietnam on his ninety-third mission, Leo Thorsness surrenders to enemy troops (above, top). He was imprisoned in the infamous North Vietnamese prison camp, the Hanoi Hilton, for six years, subjected to solitary confinement, and paraded in public (above) because he was considered a troublemaker.

Leo Thorsness and other POWs were sometimes filmed and broadcast on foreign news programs.

Leo in uniform with his Medal of Honor in 1973, after all the POWs had been released. Altogether, there are 258 recipients from the Vietnam War.

other hand: heads. In my mind, that meant the guard got tails. Neither he nor I had control of our parents, when or where we were born. Just by the accident of birth I got to be an American and he got to be North Vietnamese. He was condemned to live in a system that tortures prisoners, some of them to death. I was handed freedom, human rights, and individual opportunity. As I peeked out of the peephole in my cell, I felt blessed.

Seemingly unbearable situations come up in every life, most of them less dramatic or painful than what I experienced. You survive by asserting ownership over your life in terms of the small things, the things you can control even when you can't control the big ones. You survive hard times by using your mind and your imagination and by thinking about the good things you've had. You survive and succeed by focusing your mind on your life goals and never giving up.

Never give up.

THOMAS NORRIS AND MICHAEL THORNTON

DEVILS WITH GREEN FACES

**"We have a love for each other
greater than brothers."**

Teamwork is essential in every aspect of the military. And the more important the mission, the more important the teamwork becomes. Nowhere is this truer than in the elite navy unit known as the SEALs (short for Sea, Air, and Land teams). The SEALs are now legendary for their fights against Middle Eastern terrorists. They were the ones who killed Osama bin Laden, the mastermind of the 9/11 terrorist attacks. But long before that, they set the gold standard of teamwork under extreme conditions. And two of them, Thomas Norris and Michael Thornton, made military history in Vietnam and survived a life-and-death struggle that bonded them forever.

President John F. Kennedy established the U.S. Navy SEALs in 1962 as an elite force that would be the naval equivalent of the Army's Green Berets. In the Vietnam War, the SEALs came to play a key role, operating stealthily in small teams on the rivers, deltas, and canals that ran through-out the country. They went on secret missions to set up ambushes, disrupt enemy communications, and stage raids to capture high-value intelligence targets. The North Vietnamese learned to fear and respect the SEALs, call-ing them "devils with the green faces" because of the camouflage makeup they used as war paint on their missions.

★   ★   ★

At the height of the war, there were more than three hundred SEALs in Vietnam. But by 1972, as the United States began large-scale troop withdrawals from the country, there were only a dozen or so of these special operators left. The SEALs' mission now was mainly rescuing U.S. airmen who had been shot down and doing "sneak-and-peek" raids to keep track of the advance of North Vietnamese troops into South Vietnam. Tommy Norris and Mike Thornton were part of these actions.

Tommy's Story

Although Mike would wind up playing the role of big brother, Tommy was the older of the two by a few years. Growing up in Jacksonville, Florida, he was an Eagle Scout and a natural leader. He was lean and wiry, but stronger than he looked, and he became a conference wrestling champion at the University of Maryland. After graduating from college in 1967, he enlisted in the Navy. He had always wanted to be a pilot, even going so far as to imagine exactly the plane he would fly: the carrier-based A-4 Skyhawk, the Navy's principal fighter in the early stages of the Vietnam War. But he failed the depth-perception part of the aviator vision test, and instead of flying a Skyhawk, he decided to become a SEAL.

The SEAL training was notoriously difficult: Only about one-quarter of those who entered the six-month Basic Underwater Demolition/SEAL training course graduated. Tommy graduated from the course in 1969 and was immediately assigned to a SEAL team.

Tommy was on his second tour of duty in Vietnam in the spring of 1972 when he volunteered for the mission that would make him a legend in the SEAL community. An air force lieutenant colonel named Iceal "Gene" Hambleton was on board a U.S. electronic surveillance aircraft on a mission to jam North Vietnamese radar transmissions and communications signals when it was hit by an enemy surface-to-air missile on April 2. Hambleton was the only member of the six-man crew who ejected safely. But as his parachute drifted down into the jungle, he realized he would land in the middle of thirty thousand North Vietnamese troops staging an offensive.

At fifty-three, Hambleton was far too old to be in a combat zone. But he was also far from an average serviceman. For years he had worked in the United States as a ballistic missile expert with a top-secret air force clearance. He had volunteered for a tour of duty in Vietnam to see how weapons systems employing advanced radar worked in real-life situations. If captured, he would be a valuable intelligence asset for the North Vietnamese and even more for their Soviet backers, who would do whatever was necessary to get the classified information he had. For this reason the United States made recovering Hambleton a top priority.

Search and Rescue #1

Once on the ground, Hambleton hid by day and moved at night as he tried to evade heavy concentrations of enemy troops. The emergency radio he carried with him was his lifeline, allowing him to maintain contact with the forces trying to coordinate his recovery. This was the longest and costliest search-and-rescue mission of the Vietnam War. In the first eight days, one U.S. Army helicopter and five Air Force aircraft searching for him were shot down; ten airmen were killed, two were captured, and three more were forced to bail out, requiring rescue themselves. Alarmed at the

South Vietnamese commando Nguyen Van Kiet (left) with Tommy Norris (right). He was later awarded a U.S. Navy Cross, the only member of the South Vietnamese military ever to receive one.

losses, commanding U.S. General Creighton Abrams finally ordered that there would be no more air rescue efforts, only ground operations to find Hambleton and bring him home.

Tommy was chosen for this mission. But first he had to try to find 1st Lieutenant Mark Clark, one of the airmen shot down trying to locate Hambleton.

On the morning of April 10, Tommy, in charge of a team of five South Vietnamese commandos, was taken by an armored personnel carrier to a forward operating base (FOB) staffed by South Vietnamese soldiers. As night fell, he led the team deep into enemy territory. Lieutenant Clark had been radioed by his air controller to head to the Mieu Giang River after dark and float downstream to a point where Tommy and his men would extract him.

"We were working in and out of enemy units all night long until we finally found an area where we could watch for him," Tommy later recalled. "It was probably about two in the morning when he passed our location. I could hear him coming. He was breathing hard. But we also had a North Vietnamese patrol that was coming through. I'm sitting there praying that Clark's breathing isn't going to alert them."

After the patrol finally passed by, Tommy entered the water to look for Clark, but was unable to locate him in the dark. He notified their forward operating base to have Clark hold his position and, then, with his team, began a search, locating him near daybreak. His team took the airman back to the forward operating base. But soon after he arrived, the base was hit by a sudden enemy attack. Half the South Vietnamese soldiers there were killed before Tommy was able to organize a defense and fight off the assault.

Search and Rescue #2

For the next two days, Tommy and his men turned their attention to finding Lieutenant Colonel Hambleton. He had now been on the run

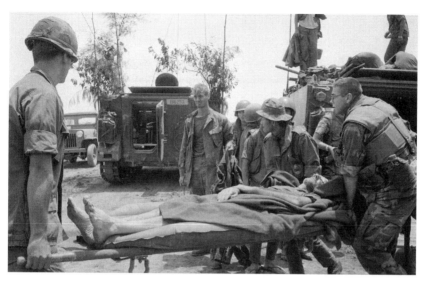

Weakened from his ordeal, Lieutenant Iceal Hambleton is loaded onto a helicopter for transport to safety in the most famous rescue operation of the war. (Tommy Norris is second from the left.)

for nine days, without food and water, watching from his hiding places as the planes searching for him were shot down. His situation was now getting critical. With each passing day he became less able to do the hard work of survival. The air controller who had been in contact with him during this time told Tommy: "This guy's not making it. He's not making his calls on schedule. When he does call, he can't talk. We dropped a survival pack, but he can't get to it. He's losing it."

Tommy decided to make a final effort, this time taking only one man with him. He asked one of the South Vietnamese commandos, Nguyen Van Kiet, if he wanted to come. "If you go, I'll go," said Kiet, who would become the only member of the South Vietnamese military ever awarded a U.S. Navy Cross for his role in the mission. "Okay," Tommy replied. "But I'm not sure either one of us is coming back."

On the night of April 12, the two men walked with stealth to an abandoned village where they found a sampan, a flat-bottomed boat used by the locals to navigate the river. In disguise, one as a native fisherman and the other as a North Vietnamese soldier, they paddled upriver. Tommy didn't know where Hambleton was hiding, but he had been given general coordinates by the Air Force, and he headed in that direction. He and Kiet passed silently by enemy units encamped near the river, including an armored unit refueling the tanks of their vehicles. They passed close enough in one case to hear enemy fighters snoring in their sleep.

After coming out of a heavy fog at daybreak, Tommy and Kiet headed downstream, and Tommy beached the sampan near the coordinates he had been given. After a brief search, he located Hambleton hiding nearby. "He realized I was an American and wanted to talk," Tommy later recalled. "I kept trying to keep him quiet, put a couple of life vests on him, put him in the bottom of the sampan and covered him with bamboo and vegetation."

Because Hambleton had been so weakened by his ordeal, Tommy didn't wait for darkness to begin the trip back to base but started down the river immediately. They were seen by a North Vietnamese patrol, which they evaded, and passed by enemy positions on the shore. They were nearing the forward operating base when they came under heavy enemy machine-gun fire. Tommy called in an air strike, and as American planes dropped bombs and smoke, he finally brought Hambleton to safety.

Tommy's superiors told him that they were going to recommend him for the Medal of Honor and asked him to write a report giving the details of the rescue. At first, he refused. "It was a mission that had to be accomplished," he said. "And somebody else in my position would have attempted to do the same thing."

Mike's Story

Six months later, after he accomplished what would become the most famous rescue of the Vietnam War, Tommy volunteered to lead a five-man SEAL patrol on what he thought would be a far more routine mission gathering intelligence in enemy territory. Along with him were three South Vietnamese commandos and another SEAL named Mike Thornton.

· BORN 1949, GREENVILLE, SOUTH CAROLINA
· ENLISTED IN U.S. NAVY, 1967
· RANK: PETTY OFFICER
· SERVICE AS NAVY SEAL IN VIETNAM, 1972
· RECEIVED MEDAL OF HONOR, 1973

THORNTON

Mike's father had worked in a cotton mill in South Carolina since the age of eleven, but he encouraged Mike to dream big. And what Mike dreamed about was becoming a SEAL. When he was a boy, he had gone to see *The Frogmen,* a 1950s movie about U.S. underwater demolition teams in Korea, and decided that this was what he wanted to do. Built like a football linebacker, he had made himself a powerful swimmer. He joined the Navy right out of high school in 1967, served as a gunner's mate on board destroyers for a year until he entered water demolition recruit training, and became one of twelve members of his class of 129 chosen for the SEALs.

Mike was not only younger than Tommy, now his commanding officer, but he was also more easygoing and impulsive. He had been eager for action since he arrived in Vietnam on New Year's Day 1970 as a SEAL. As one of his comrades said, "Mike never met a mission he didn't like."

When the mission led by Tommy began on the morning of October 31, the fact that it was Halloween passed through Mike's mind and made him smile as he painted his face with camouflage. The patrol's objective was to capture prisoners and gather intelligence from an enemy base. The base was situated strategically on the Cua Viet River near the seacoast, just south of the DMZ (demilitarized zone), which had been established as a boundary between North and South Vietnam during the mid-1950s.

The team approached the coast by sea in a South Vietnamese junk, a seagoing ship used in Asia for hundreds of years. The SEALs transferred to a rubber boat, paddled to within a mile of the shoreline, and swam the rest of the way, crawling onto the beach in the middle of the night and then moving silently inland.

Navy SEAL Mike Thornton in full dress uniform, with combat and service medals, including the Medal of Honor, following his promotion to Navy lieutenant in the 1970s.

As Mike later recalled the scene, "Tommy's on point. We've got the three Vietnamese in the middle. And I'm rear security." As the sun came up, they saw that the area they were passing through was more heavily armed and populated than the base that was supposed to be their objective. They realized that because of a navigation error, they had landed too far north and were actually inside North Vietnam.

"To our south we could see this village," Mike remembered later. "We heard dogs barking and stuff like that. We wanted to get as far away as we could." Tommy ordered the patrol to head toward the ocean. "We went through about four sets of sand dunes," Mike recalled. "And we came to this one gigantic dune that stood by itself." They decided to hide there while Tommy radioed for help.

At this point, a pair of enemy soldiers came walking toward them, single file. They hadn't yet seen the SEAL patrol but were heading right for it. Keeping his cover, Mike motioned for Thai, one of the South Vietnamese commandos, to follow him as he scrambled about a hundred yards through the dunes to get closer to the North Vietnamese. Mike handed Thai a "hush puppy," a .22 caliber pistol with a silencer, and pointed at the lead enemy soldier: "When I take this guy out, I want you to sneak up behind the other guy and eliminate him," he whispered.

As the first soldier came near, Mike stood up and hit him on the head with the butt of his rifle, knocking him out. Then he motioned for Thai to shoot the other one. Instead, Thai stood up and yelled, in Vietnamese, "Stop! Come here!" The soldier, armed with an AK-47,

A SEAL unit in camouflage hits the water after exiting a Navy landing craft, 1967. The Navy SEALs served an important role in the Vietnam War, often conducting dangerous missions to gather intelligence behind enemy lines.

sprayed several shots at Thai, then began running toward the village. Mike followed, kneeling along the trail to take a long-distance shot, which killed the soldier. But by now, the entire village had been awakened by the noise, and Mike saw about fifty enemy fighters grab their weapons and head toward his position.

As the North Vietnamese charged them, Tommy shot a rocket-propelled grenade, which exploded in the tree line and slowed down the enemy for a moment. Then the attacking force split up into several groups and started trying to surround the SEAL patrol. Tommy held his position with two of the South Vietnamese commandos, a man named Dang and another named Da Wei. Mike dug in with Thai a hundred yards away as a violent firefight erupted.

Mike estimated that the team had killed about thirty of the enemy over the next few hours when a grenade suddenly landed near him on a sand dune. He quickly rolled over, but the blast peppered his back with shrapnel. "I could hear Tommy yelling, 'Mike! Mike!' Four guys came over the top of this sand dune, and I shot all of them."

Finding Tommy

As Mike made sure the four North Vietnamese were dead, Dang ran toward him from the other SEAL position. He yelled to Mike that Tommy and Da Wei were both dead and that he and Mike and Thai had to run for their lives. Mike shook his head. "No, I'll go back for Tommy."

> **Mike shook his head. "No, I'll go back for Tommy."**

Mike ordered Dang and Thai to provide covering fire as enemy bullets kicked up the sand all around him. "I got to the position where Tommy was," Mike later said. "He was lying on the side of a dune. And five guys are coming after him. I killed those five guys and grabbed Tommy and put him on my shoulders."

Tommy had been shot in the forehead. His skull was shattered and he was barely clinging to life. Before he was hit, seeing that the SEAL team would have to get back to the water to survive, he had radioed an American battle cruiser standing offshore to wait five minutes for the team to get clear and then begin firing on their position. Those shells were now starting to hit all around Mike as he ran with Tommy toward the water, firing at the pursuing enemy as he went.

Mike was out of ammunition when he carried Tommy into the ocean. "As we swam through the surf zone, you could see the bullets just going through the water, like in a movie. I looked over to my right, and there's little Dang floundering in the water, shot through his right hip. He couldn't swim, so I grabbed him and had him wrap his arms around me."

Supporting Tommy and Dang, Mike began swimming the breaststroke out to sea. He swam for approximately three hours before being picked up by the junk that had delivered the team sixteen hours earlier. The men were taken back to the American destroyers and from there to Da Nang Air Base. Tommy was put on an emergency flight to the Philippines, where he underwent a nineteen-hour operation, the first of more than a dozen painful medical procedures he would undergo over the next three years.

Two Medals

Tommy was still in the naval hospital, in Bethesda, Maryland, undergoing facial reconstruction surgery and being fitted for an artificial eye when Mike was to receive the Medal of Honor on October 15, 1973. Doctors had ordered Tommy not to attend the ceremony, but Mike snuck into the hospital on his way to the White House, carried him out the back door, and took him along.

Two and a half years later, on March 6, 1976, Mike was again at the White House, this time sitting in the front row as Tommy received his own medal for the rescue of Lieutenant Mark Clark Jr. and Lieutenant Colonel Iceal Hambleton. The award had been delayed for several years because that top secret mission to recover Hambleton was still classified.

When his medical condition stabilized, Tommy joined the FBI after proving that he was capable of doing the job despite the injuries he had suffered. Mike continued to serve as a SEAL until his retirement from the military in 1980. The two men have remained close through the years, united by unforgettable events on a fire-swept beach in a faraway place and a bygone time. "We have a love for each other greater than brothers," said Mike.

Proud Navy SEAL Mike Thornton after receiving the Medal of Honor from President Richard Nixon. He made sure his wounded buddy Tommy Norris was at the White House to witness the ceremony.

SEAL TRAINING: *The Toughest and the Best*

To carry out the most dangerous missions in the U.S. military—jumping out of planes, swimming long distances in treacherous waters, stalking the enemy silently, and surviving under any conditions—Navy SEALs train for six grueling months, making them among the toughest men alive. Only about 25 percent of those who begin this program graduate and become SEALs.

Candidates for Basic Underwater Demolition/SEAL must:

· Go on distance runs in the mountains wearing forty-five-pound packs and complete two-mile ocean swims and four-mile runs in the sand—all within time limits.

· Dive down fifty feet and tie a complex nautical knot.

· Show they're "drown-proof" by entering a nine-foot-deep pool with their hands and legs tied, then bob—sinking to the bottom of the pool and kicking up with their toes to catch a breath at the surface of the water—for five

The SEAL training program, which subjects candidates to almost unendurable physical and mental challenges, is designed to eliminate those who wouldn't be able to operate under extreme combat conditions.

minutes. They also have to swim for 100 meters (almost 330 feet) using only a dolphin kick, dive to the bottom of the pool, and retrieve an object like a diving mask with their teeth.

Hell Week

Training begins with Hell Week, including "surf torture" in the icy cold of the Pacific Ocean and drills in the sand for twenty hours a day. Candidates have only a limited amount of food and just one or two hours of sleep a night.

If a candidate can't take the training any longer, he has to ring a bell outside his barracks three times, and he will be granted permission to leave the program. Each time the bell sounds, it reminds those listening that only the very best become SEALs.

Approximately 250 new SEALs graduate each year. When they receive the unit's trident pin, it is a sign that they have survived a program that emphasizes emotional strength as well as physical toughness, and that they are ready to join the military's most elite group.

The SEALs are our nation's toughest warriors. They are trained to operate in or under water, in deserts, and at high altitudes.

THE WARS IN IRAQ AND AFGHANISTAN

Campaigns Against an Elusive Enemy

The United States went to war soon after the attacks of September 11, 2001 (see pages 182–83). This was the most devastating surprise assault on the American homeland since Pearl Harbor was bombed by the Japanese in 1941. But the enemy in this case was not another nation. Instead, it was an international group of terrorists known as al-Qaeda. Soon after the attacks, President George W. Bush said, "Our war on terror will not end until every terrorist group of global reach has been found, stopped, and defeated." The targets in this war included terror organizations as well as the nations that supported them and gave them refuge.

In October 2001, the United States sent special forces into Afghanistan. Osama bin Laden, head of al-Qaeda and mastermind of the 9/11 attacks, was living there under the protection of the Taliban (see pages 142–43), an extremist Islamic group that ruled Afghanistan. The Taliban refused to hand over bin Laden to the United States. In less than a month, American soldiers, supported by the armies of local warlords in the Northern Alliance, drove the Taliban from power. Many members of bin Laden's group were killed in the first days of the U.S. assault, but bin Laden escaped. He became the subject of the most determined manhunt in American history, and he was finally discovered almost ten years later to be hiding in Pakistan. American SEAL Team 6 launched a raid on bin Laden's walled compound and killed him on May 2, 2011.

The Search for Dangerous Weapons

The next front in this war on terror was Iraq, a country controlled by the dictator Saddam Hussein. Since 1990, the United States believed that the Hussein regime supported terrorism. Hussein had used chemical weapons against his own people more than once, and the United Nations

OPPOSITE, TOP: A U.S. Army soldier mans a .50 caliber machine gun above the town of Kamdesh in eastern Afghanistan in 2012. This remote area was an important strategic position for intercepting enemy fighters and weapons coming from neighboring Pakistan.

OPPOSITE, BOTTOM: A Taliban fighter on patrol in November 2001, just weeks after U.S. special forces entered Afghanistan in an effort to remove the Taliban from power.

had punished his regime by preventing other nations from trading with Iraq. In October 2002, a large majority in the U.S. Congress authorized the use of force against Iraq. This decision was based on intelligence information—later proved to be wrong—that the Hussein regime had a large supply of weapons of mass destruction, possibly including nuclear devices. The fear was that the regime could give these weapons to terror groups for use against the United States and its allies. The war began in March 2003, and Iraq's capital city, Baghdad, fell to U.S. forces a month later.

Americans began to question the Iraq invasion when no weapons of mass destruction were discovered. Also, what appeared to be an easy victory soon became a prolonged struggle against an uprising by Iraqi extremist groups, as well as violent clashes among different factions. Over the next few years more than four thousand Americans were killed in the fighting.

In 2007, a surge of additional troops were sent to Iraq, which stabilized the situation. American combat soldiers were withdrawn from Iraq in 2011, although they continued to fight in Afghanistan, where, since the original 2001 invasion, the Taliban had regrouped and began waging a guerrilla campaign against the government throughout the country. The war in Afghanistan is already America's longest in its history.

The Islamic State

Events in Iraq and Afghanistan have shown that it is far easier to start a war than end it. After the United States withdrew from Iraq, the terror group previously known as al-Qaeda in Iraq began to gain power there. Other fighters joined them, particularly Islamic extremists who were also fighting in the civil war in neighboring Syria, which began in 2011. Al-Qaeda in Iraq renamed itself the Islamic State in Iraq and Syria (ISIS)—which it later shortened to the Islamic State (IS)—and began a terror campaign in Syria and especially in Iraq. Iraqi forces, no longer backed by American troops, were powerless to stop it.

The U.S. Navy launched its first drone from an aircraft carrier on May 14, 2013. These unmanned, armed aircraft are deployed for surveillance throughout the world wherever terrorist groups might be hiding.

The Islamic State doesn't want only to wage a terror war; it wants to control territory and to set up a worldwide Islamic extremist government. By the middle of 2014, as its strength grew to an estimated 30,000 fighters, IS had conquered large portions of Iraq, including Mosul, the country's second largest city. In the area it controlled, the Islamic State became notorious for genocidal attacks on Christians and members of other religions who refused to convert to radical Islam, and on the Kurds and other ethnic groups. IS was condemned as a terrorist organization by the United Nations, the European Union, the United States, and Japan after it beheaded Western prisoners and showed these executions on the Internet. As a result of these televised murders and the Islamic State's territorial gains, in 2014 the United States, with a coalition of allied aircraft, began an air campaign against IS in Iraq and Syria. In addition, American specialists began training select rebel groups to fight IS in Syria and advising and training Iraqi forces to fight IS in Iraq.

BRINGING
A BUDDY
HOME

"This is my chance. I can make a difference."

Salvatore Giunta was eighteen, a kid from middle America, just out of high school and working part time as a "sandwich artist" at Subway in late 2003. He had no idea what he was going to do with his life when he heard a radio commercial for the U.S. Army that would change everything.

It had been two years since the United States was attacked by Islamic terrorists on September 11, 2001. Sal's chemistry teacher had rushed a television into the classroom the morning that hijackers crashed two jets into the World Trade Center in New York City just as the second plane hit the second tower. "It was our first view of evil," Sal said.

Over the next couple of years, Sal couldn't shake the image of New Yorkers running for their lives as the towers collapsed. It stayed with him as he graduated from high school with an undistinguished record, took the job at Subway, and tried to sort out what he'd do with his life. He made an appointment with an army recruiter, telling himself he was only interested in the free T-shirt offered on the radio. But by the time he arrived at the recruitment office, he had made up his mind. He volunteered on the spot. "Here's my chance. I can make a difference," he said to himself. "I'm going to do this."

★   ★   ★

Sal's story started in another country, as so many American stories do. His great-grandfather and great-grandmother on his father's side were from Sicily; like millions of other immigrants, they came to America at the turn of the twentieth century looking for a better life. Over the next two generations, the Giuntas worked so hard at becoming American that when Sal was born in 1985, the family's Italian roots were just a pleasant memory.

Growing up in Cedar Rapids, Iowa, in "a Midwest, middle-class, sunshine, rainbows, green grass, you-do-not-have-to-lock-your-door sort of neighborhood," as Sal calls it, was everything a kid could want. Sal was popular and had many friends, but he admits that he was a mediocre student, not really interested in school and doing just well enough to get by: "I'd just sit there in class, half interested, half daydreaming—a kid who would rather have been somewhere else."

Then came 9/11, which eventually led Sal to give up his comfortable midwestern life to serve his country. It was a decision he never

Sal Giunta stands beside a military jeep. Various guns are frequently mounted on jeeps and other vehicles to provide a quick means of defense from enemy fire.

· BORN 1985, CLINTON, IOWA
· ENLISTED IN U.S. ARMY, 2003
· SERVICE IN KORENGAL VALLEY,
  AFGHANISTAN, 2007
· RANK: SPECIALIST
· UNIT: COMPANY B, 2ND BATTALION
  (AIRBORNE) 503RD INFANTRY REGIMENT;
  173RD AIRBORNE BRIGADE COMBAT TEAM
· RECEIVED MEDAL OF HONOR, 2010

SALVATORE GIUNTA

regretted. "I learned twenty valuable lessons before seven o'clock every morning when I first got in the Army," he says. A good football player in high school despite his average size, he added muscle during basic training and felt that he was ready for any challenge.

At Fort Benning, Georgia, Sal learned how to parachute out of planes as a member of the 173rd Airborne Brigade Combat Team—the Sky Soldiers—which had first distinguished itself in the Vietnam War. His first posting was at the American base in Vicenza, Italy, which gave him a chance to explore his Italian heritage during weekend leaves. While there, he also got to talk to some of the first U.S. soldiers who had fought in Iraq. The stories they told sharpened his appetite for combat. He was excited when his unit was deployed to Afghanistan in the spring of 2005; at last he'd have the chance to take revenge on the terrorists responsible for the attack on America.

The Truth About War

But Sal soon learned firsthand that while war might be about patriotic ideals, it was also about death and loss. In his first three months in Afghanistan, he saw four of his buddies killed by a roadside bomb that destroyed the truck they were riding in. "These were people in the prime of their life," he says. "They were not people who ate too much greasy food and had a heart attack. They would never be stronger than they were on that day when suddenly they had no more tomorrows. These deaths affected me. I lost some of the excitement, but I wanted to get the job done more than ever."

Sal's first tour in Afghanistan lasted for a year. In the spring of 2007, his unit returned for a second tour. This time it was helicoptered into a place called Firebase Vegas in the remote Korengal Valley, near the border with Pakistan. "It was like nothing I had ever seen in Afghanistan before," Sal recalls. "We were at the bottom of the valley, with mountains just straight up and down on every side. Every place you're going to fight, you're at the bottom and they are at the top. You're in the open and they have cover." The place was known as the Valley of Death, because so many American servicemen had died fighting there.

The place was known as the Valley of Death, because so many American servicemen had died fighting there.

Over the next few months, the soldiers at Firebase Vegas helped build roads and completed other projects to improve the lives of the locals by day and hunted the "bad guys" in night raids. On October 23, 2007, his company was at the end of a five-day-long mission to clear out groups of Taliban fighters before winter arrived when the enemy overran one of the company's reconnaissance patrols, killing a staff sergeant and wounding two other Americans. Sal and the others had heard it happen on their radios. "We were only a kilometer away," he remembers. "We were listening to a million bad things happening to our brothers."

Two days later, when word came that the Taliban were showing off the weapons and equipment they had taken during this firefight as "war trophies" in a local village, Sal's company commander ordered two platoons to get it back. Sal's platoon took a position on a mountain ridge overlooking the town to provide cover for this mission.

Ambush!

Shortly after nightfall, the U.S. equipment in the village had been recovered without incident, and Sal's eight-man platoon was ordered to return to base. Their way lit by the full moon, they had walked for about five minutes and entered an open area when rocket-propelled grenades and machine-gun fire suddenly began to explode all around them. There were a few shrubs and bushes, but nothing that would stop a bullet.

Sergeant Joshua Brennan was wounded when Taliban fighters ambushed his platoon in 2007. Sal rescued his friend from enemy hands and returned him to American lines.

The platoon had walked into an L-shaped ambush, in which the enemy was along one side and ahead of them.

The gunfire was more intense than anything Sal had ever experienced. "There were more bullets in the air than stars in the sky," he later said. "They're above you, in front of you, behind you, below you. They're hitting in the dirt; they're going over your head. They were close—close as I've ever seen." Apache helicopter gunships were circling above the action, but the Americans and Taliban were so close together that the aircraft couldn't open fire for fear of hitting their own men.

Sergeant Joshua Brennan was leading the platoon when the firing erupted. He was hit several times and fell to the ground. Specialist Hugo Mendoza, the squad medic, rushed forward to help Brennan, but was himself shot and killed. Sal saw squad leader Erick Gallardo's helmet jerk as he, too, went down. Fearing that Gallardo had been shot in the head, Sal ran through heavy fire to get to him. But the bullet had only bounced off Gallardo's helmet. Sal pulled him back to a small depression in the ground, maybe six inches deep, where the two of them lay as flat as possible. An enemy round hit Sal in the chest, but his protective vest stopped it. Another bullet, that otherwise would have hit him in the neck, struck the rocket launcher he was carrying over his left shoulder and shattered it.

Realizing that the Taliban fighters were on the verge of overrunning the unit, Sal stood up and counterattacked. "I am throwing my grenades," he recalls. "I only had three with me, and then there were no more grenades and I was running forward toward the shooting."

Sal frantically looked for Sergeant Brennan as he charged ahead, not knowing how badly he was hurt but hoping to drag him back to safety. He and Josh Brennan were close friends. They had traveled through Italy on weekends when their unit was stationed at Vicenza and had served side by side on both tours in Afghanistan.

Finding a Friend

But Joshua was not where he had fallen when hit by a volley of enemy bullets. Searching for his friend, Sal sprinted through some low shrubs and into a clearing he later described as a "scary, empty, flat space." In the distance, he made out the forms of what he thought at first were three men running away. But then he realized that it was actually two Taliban fighters who were dragging a third man—Sergeant Brennan. "This part

In Afghanistan's Korengal Valley, Sal Giunta's platoon is in full desert camouflage. The men are carrying their personal weapons for rapid response against surprise attacks.

haunts my dreams," Sal says. "Joshua is like a brother to me. He's smarter than me and stronger than me, faster than me, and a better shot. But here, he's the one getting carried away."

Firing as he ran forward to get his friend, Sal killed one of the Taliban and wounded the other, who dropped Sergeant Brennan and limped off. Sal reached his buddy, picked him up, and carried him back to the open space where the other members of his squad had set up a defensive position. He quickly examined Joshua: "I think he was shot maybe seven times, and maybe a rocket-propelled grenade hit the ground nearby and shrapnel had taken off part of his jaw." Sal called for Mendoza, the squad's medic, not knowing that he'd already been killed. He tried to reassure Joshua that he'd make it, as he and the other GIs gave him medical aid. "You'll get out and you'll tell hero stories," he yelled to his friend above the battle-field din. Joshua nodded weakly.

> "Joshua is like a brother to me. He's smarter than me and stronger than me, faster than me, and a better shot."

By the time the medevac helicopter arrived for Sergeant Brennan, the Taliban had melted away into the night. Sal and his unit walked two and a half hours back to the base. It was one o'clock in the morning and they were eating their first hot food in days when the company commander came into the mess hall. He told them that everyone else was going to be okay, but that Joshua Brennan had died. "That was my hell," Sal remembers. "That was my bad day."

Singled Out for an Honor

A week or so later, Sal learned that he had been recommended for the Medal of Honor. At that time, six other U.S. servicemen had received the award for heroism in Iraq and Afghanistan, but all of them had been killed in action. Sal would be the first living recipient of the medal in forty years, since the last days of the war in Vietnam.

In the three years it took for the recommendation to be investigated and approved, Sal sometimes felt a kind of dread—not only because he knew that receiving the medal would change his life, but also because he believed that all the others involved in that fight in the Korengal Valley were as worthy of the honor as he was. He felt uncomfortable being singled out. "I got congratulated and patted on the back and kissed and loved," he says. "But it hurt because I know that there are guys who will never get congratulations or thank-yous or see their family or their children." The only consolation was that the last thing his friend Joshua Brennan had seen was Sal and his other buddies taking care of him. Brennan had not died in enemy hands.

President Barack Obama fastened the medal around Sal's neck at the White House on October 25, 2010. "I can say at the end of my life that I fought for this country the best I knew how, and the Medal of Honor represents that," Sal said at the time. "It represents everyone who left their life behind wherever they were—in Iowa or New York or California or Florida—to do something not for themselves but for their country. It's about people who did that yesterday, are doing it today, and will be doing it again tomorrow. No matter how bad things are, no matter how big their losses are, they will continue to do it because that's what makes America great."

In 2010 President Barack Obama awarded the Medal of Honor to Sal Giunta, who was the first living person since the Vietnam War to receive the U.S. military's highest decoration for valor.

WHO ARE THE TALIBAN?

The Taliban are a group of terrorists in Afghanistan who practice an extreme form of the Islamic religion that condones the killing of "infidels" (nonbelievers and Westerners). Every aspect of life under the Taliban is regulated. Men are forced to grow beards, and everything about women's lives—from how they look to where they are allowed to go—is controlled by male authorities. Television, movies—even video games—are forbidden. Those who fail to obey are subject to severe punishments, from chopping off the hands of those accused of stealing to beheading those who question Islam.

The Taliban began as a group of a few dozen fanatical students in Afghanistan who fought the Soviet Union when it occupied their country from 1979 to 1989. After the Soviet Union withdrew, the Taliban continued to fight against other Afghan groups for control of the country, which it took in 1996.

Strict Rules for Daily Life

While in power, the Taliban enforced a rigid form of Sharia—Islamic law that governs every detail of daily social life. Under its brutal rule, harmless activities, such as listening to music, playing chess, and flying kites, were banned. Public executions of lawbreakers were held in sports arenas. Women were forced to wear full-length burkas—black garments covering them from head to toe, with only a slit for their eyes. If they left the house without a male escort, they were beaten by the religious police who patrolled the country's streets. A woman caught wearing nail polish might have the tips of her fingers cut off.

Believing that Islam was in a war against the West and its democratic values, the Taliban allowed Osama bin Laden's al-Qaeda, a terror group that had launched attacks against the United States around the world in the 1990s, to set up a headquarters in Afghanistan, where it planned the 9/11 attacks.

A month after those attacks, U.S. Special Forces moved into Afghanistan. Fighting alongside tribal groups who opposed the Taliban, they forced them

A group of Taliban fighters. Many weapons used by the Taliban, such as the rocket-propelled grenade and the A-K 47, were developed in the Soviet Union and used against the Afghan population during the Soviet occupation of Afghanistan in the 1980s.

out of power that same year. Most of the Taliban leaders hid in neighboring Pakistan and waited for an opportunity to resume their fight.

That opportunity came after the United States invaded Iraq in 2003. While America focused its attention there, the Taliban took up arms once again. In 2004, Afghanistan held its first democratic election (with women casting 40 percent of the ballots) even though the Taliban threatened to kill anyone who voted. The United States backed the newly elected central government, and the Taliban re-formed into a guerrilla force.

The Taliban has fought against the elected government of Afghanistan and U.S. forces for more than a decade. By 2014, an estimated thirty thousand Taliban had been killed, while twenty-three hundred Americans, along with nearly fifteen thousand Afghan government troops, had also died in this war, the longest in U.S. history.

BORN
TO FIGHT

"Your actions are what make you."

When Staff Sergeant Clint Romesha (pronounced *Rome-uh-shay*) arrived at Outpost Keating in Afghanistan in the summer of 2009, he felt that for the first time in nearly ten years in the Army, doing mostly noncombat jobs, he was in a place where anything could happen.

Clint and his men were now in the most dangerous spot in the most dangerous country for an American soldier, and they were badly outnumbered by the Taliban. The fight for Outpost Keating would be one of the most fearsome of the Afghan war, and Clint would be at the center of it. He seemed destined to be there.

★ ★ ★

Named for Benjamin Keating, an American officer who had been killed there in 2006, the outpost was near the town of Kamdesh in a remote and desolate province in eastern Afghanistan on the Pakistan border.

Clint was struck by how vulnerable the American position was—a few prefabricated buildings sitting in a bowl at the base of three steep mountains so dense with trees that they were perfect cover for snipers and staging areas for enemy attacks. The roads from the closest big city, Jalalabad, were narrow, poorly constructed, and filled with the carcasses of American trucks and Humvees ambushed there over the years. Taliban fighters hiding in the ridges above let loose rocket-propelled grenades and heavy machine-gun fire when the helicopters carrying most of the camp's supplies appeared. The pilots had begun limiting their flights to moonless nights when the darkness offered at least a little protection.

The outpost was designed as a place where U.S. forces could intercept enemy fighters and weapons coming in from Pakistan. Another part of the mission there was "counterinsurgency"—an effort to improve the lives of local tribesmen and convince them that it was in their interests to oppose the Taliban. As part of this counterinsurgency effort in Kamdesh, the Army had spent millions building schools, electricity grids, water systems, and other improvements.

But winning the hearts and minds of the locals had been an uphill struggle. Most people around Kamdesh were illiterate, opposed to their country's central government, and suspicious of all outsiders. And because the Taliban had murdered many of the tribal leaders who cooperated with U.S. reconstruction projects, local residents became afraid to continue to participate in the program. Soon after Clint arrived at Outpost Keating, an official army study concluded that because counterinsurgency efforts had failed, there were more enemy fighters in the area and the outpost was "indefensible." A decision was made to close it.

Clint Romesha (center) with his men at Outpost Keating in eastern Afghanistan.

· BORN 1981, LAKE CITY, CALIFORNIA
· ENLISTED IN U.S. ARMY, 1999
· RANK: STAFF SERGEANT
· UNIT: BRAVO TROOP, 3-61ST CAVALRY, 4TH
  BRIGADE COMBAT TEAM, 4TH INFANTRY
· SERVICE AT OUTPOST KEATING, NURISTAN
  PROVINCE, AFGHANISTAN, 2009
· SEPARATED FROM ARMY, 2011
· RECEIVED MEDAL OF HONOR, 2013

IN ROMESHA

All in the Family

Clint understood the dangers he faced at Outpost Keating. But he also felt that he had been born to fight in such a difficult situation. His grandfather had been an army combat engineer in World War II and had distinguished himself in the Battle of the Bulge. His father had done two tours of duty in Vietnam. His two older brothers joined the military. As a kid in the tiny northern California town of Lake City (population 60)—a place so small, Clint liked to joke, that "it was hard to find a girl to date who wasn't related to you"—he had thought of the military as a family business where he would someday have a job, too.

As a teenager, Clint longed to be a basketball player, but because he was short and wiry he became a soccer player instead. His friends saw him as someone with an edgy sense of humor who thought that actions were more important than words. "My granddaddy taught me that you tell someone you're going to do something, you do it," he liked to say. "Your actions are what make you."

Clint joined the Army shortly after his eighteenth birthday in 1999. He trained as a gunner for the M1 Abrams tank and was sent to Germany. Two weeks later, his armored battalion was reassigned to Kosovo in the Balkans as part of a NATO peacekeeping force. (Their mission was to keep the war that Serbia had fought against the Albanian population of this area from resuming.) His unit was given the mission of protecting the mass graves of civilians killed by the Serbians. "The only shooting we did," Clint recalled, "was of wild dogs that dug up these burial sites."

Clint returned to Germany in 2000. It was there that he saw the attack on the World Trade Center on TV, and later watched U.S. Special Forces enter Afghanistan to root out the Taliban terrorists who had supported the attack. He wanted to get in the fight, but the mountains of Afghanistan were no place for tanks.

Instead, Clint was sent to South Korea for fifteen months, and then to Iraq in 2004. He came home to Fort Carson, Colorado, in 2008 and was retrained as a cavalry scout operating in hunter-killer teams to collect information on the enemy and engage it in small mobile units. As he put it, he learned "to get light and how to sneak around."

Test of Bravery

When his commanders told Clint's unit that it was being sent to Outpost Keating, they frankly admitted that it was a dangerous assignment. In the three years the outpost existed, many American soldiers had been killed. "We knew it was going to be hairy," Clint later said. "But true-grit soldiers do what they have to do."

Outpost Keating was manned by about fifty U.S. soldiers and another thirty-five or so Afghan government troops. Clint said, "We were getting hit at least once a day. Those were probably efforts to test our ability to react. When I was in Iraq, I hadn't been impressed by the enemy. But these Taliban fighters were well trained. They knew how long they had to attack us before our air support arrived."

Local Afghans had been telling the Americans for days that many more Taliban than usual had entered the area. But with no electronic intelligence to back up the warnings, the camp commanders ignored them. Then, at 6:00 a.m. on October 3, 2009, about three hundred enemy fighters launched a carefully coordinated attack that began with rocket-propelled grenades and heavy machine-gun fire.

"At the beginning it was the zip and ping of bullets and sudden destruction," Clint recalls. He understood immediately that the enemy was probing for weak

Clint on leave with his infant son.

spots where it could break through the American defenses and enter the outpost. The Taliban began by destroying the American mortar position, which had the only weapons capable of firing effectively into the staging areas in the mountains. Small groups of heavily armed enemy fighters then rushed Outpost Keating's defensive perimeter.

"In heavy contact!" the outpost's command center radioed the U.S. base in Jalalabad, which radioed back that helicopter gunships had taken off but were at least forty minutes away.

Clint saw most of the Afghan government soldiers throw down their weapons and slink away as the fighting began, some hiding and others joining the Taliban. He heard over his radio that Americans were pinned down throughout the main compound, some wounded and some dead. As a staff sergeant, he was one of the most visible leaders at the outpost. Now, moving through the enemy fire, he tried to deploy his men at key positions to keep the post from being overrun.

Two Apache helicopter gunships finally arrived and began spraying the enemy with their machine guns. The Taliban opened fire on them with the heavy weapons they had hidden in the mountains. One of the Apaches was hit and forced to return to base. The pilot of the other one, seeing the Taliban advance as the outnumbered U.S. troops pulled back, radioed Jalalabad that the situation was "potentially catastrophic."

About two hours after the battle began, the Taliban finally breached Outpost Keating's defenses and set many of the buildings, constructed of flammable plywood, on fire. They were now coming through the compound's front gate. Realizing that the situation was critical, Clint and his assistant gunner ran to the barracks, grabbed an MK 48 machine gun, and then headed for the camp's generator to use it for cover. Clint destroyed a machine-gun position that had been cutting down U.S. troops. But a rocket-propelled grenade slammed into the generator, and shrapnel shredded his upper body.

Clint checked to make sure his gunner was okay and moved to another position. A soldier fighting beside him quickly put a bandage over the large hole in Clint's arm to stop the bleeding. Disregarding his wounds, Clint thought to himself, "We need to retake this compound now!" Having left the machine gun back at the generator, he picked up a rifle he saw lying on the ground and opened fire on an enemy position on the hill above the compound. He destroyed it, then killed three enemy fighters running toward him.

Clint remembers feeling oddly focused in the confusion of the gunfight: "When things get chaotic, I've always been able to break them down into their basic elements instead of getting overwhelmed. The strange thing was that as this battle progressed, I felt I was finally doing my job. I was getting my ultimate manhood test. It was time for us to shine and show what we could do."

> **Disregarding his wounds, Clint thought to himself, "We need to retake this compound now!"**

A group of Taliban approached the ammunition depot, whose doors had been destroyed. Clint knew that if they took control of the building, it could mean that the badly outnumbered American force would be wiped out.

Clint ran inside one of the barracks being used as a defensive position and asked for volunteers to save the depot. Five men stood up, and one of them called out, "We'll follow you anywhere." With Clint leading the way, the small squad ran through heavy fire to the corner of the ammunition depot, mowing down several Taliban fighters coming at them.

Pushing Back

As Clint directed his team's fire and dodged sniper bullets all around him, the Americans slowly pushed the enemy away from the building. When he got to the depot doorway, he radioed the outpost's command center to tell an approaching U.S. fighter-bomber to drop its load as close as possible, because the enemy was only a few yards away from his men. Clint's actions allowed the Americans fighting from various positions in the compound to regroup and retake the initiative. As they began to move forward, he provided cover for three wounded Americans trying to get to the aid station. Then he rushed into heavy fire to recover the bodies of two of his fallen comrades, so that the Taliban couldn't carry them away as trophies of war.

"I knew we had some momentum and had to keep pushing," Clint explained. "We advanced on the enemy, using heavy fire to back them out of the front gate. We tossed smoke grenades and used the cover they provided to close the gate."

By 6:00 p.m., after twelve hours of fighting, the Battle of Kamdesh, as it would become known, was over. Eight American soldiers were dead,

U.S. soldiers fire a 120mm mortar at a Taliban position from a combat outpost in Kunar, in eastern Afghanistan. Mortar fire, often with helicopter backup, was one of several offensive tactics used against the enemy.

making it one of the bloodiest battles of the war. The U.S. forces had killed an estimated 150 Taliban fighters.

Three days later, the entire U.S. force evacuated Outpost Keating by helicopter. "We had rigged all the buildings with explosives set to go off thirty minutes after we left," Clint recalls. "But they didn't go off. An Air Force B-1 bomber finished the job." Afterward, aerial photographs showed only faint indentations in the ground where buildings had once stood.

At the White House

A year and a half after the battle, Clint left the Army to spend more time with his wife and children. He settled in North Dakota and took a job in the oil industry. In October 2011, he received a call from Washington informing him that he was to be awarded the Medal of Honor.

When Clint arrived at the White House for the medal ceremony on February 11, 2013, First Lady Michelle Obama asked him to be her guest at the State of the Union address sched-

For his actions in the twelve-hour battle of Kamdesh despite being badly wounded, Staff Sergeant Romesha received the Medal of Honor in 2013 from President Barack Obama.

uled for the following evening. He accepted the invitation, but after President Obama put the medal around his neck in front of a group that included not only his family but also many of the men he had served with at Outpost Keating and the wives and children of some who had died there, he whispered to the president that on second thought he'd rather spend the evening with the people who had stood with him on that day in Kamdesh.

Some of the details about the Battle of Kamdesh are from *The Outpost: An Untold Story of American Valor,* by Jake Tapper (Little, Brown and Co., 2012).

It happened on a routine mission in Iraq: A roadside bomb exploded and forever changed the lives of a soldier and her family. Mother and daughter both give their accounts, each from her own point of view.

War Wounds That Last a Lifetime

BY JUANITA MILLIGAN

In the summer of 2005, I was an army platoon sergeant in the 465th Transportation Company in Balad, Iraq. Our job was hauling ammunition, food, and supplies to our troops all over Iraq. Our convoys consisted of twenty tractor-trailer trucks with civilian drivers protected by four heavily up-armored Humvees with three soldiers in each, including a gunner operating a large-caliber machine gun mounted on the roof. I was always concerned when we were on a mission, but there was some comfort in the layer of metal between us and the unseen bombs we knew were hidden along the roads we traveled.

On the morning of August 20, I had a momentary thought that something might go wrong. I quickly dismissed it, but sure enough, midway through our mission, one of these roadside bombs ripped through the passenger side of our vehicle where I was sitting. Everything turned to slow motion. I remember seeing the debris raining down on our windshield. Training kicked in, and I started looking out for my teammates and assessing our situation. Not realizing how bad my injuries were, I reached up for our gunner who was partially exposed to the fury of the blast, wanting to help him, unsure if he was alive. Thankfully he was okay, but I wasn't. Shrapnel had severed two nerves in my upper arm, taking soft tissue with it. The explosion had blown more shrapnel through my seat, crushing my femur and taking a chunk out of my leg. Shock wore off and pain rushed in.

In a past war, my life would have ended on the hot asphalt in Iraq. But improved medical technology—and the

Master Sergeant Juanita Milligan.

bravery of my three comrades, who drove me in another Humvee to the forward operating base—gave me a second chance. Thinking of my children kept me alive as we raced down that highway toward an aid station. The bumpy ride of recovery I took them on over the next few years would be filled with heartache and worry about the way their lives had been altered. They learned, as I did, that not all the wounds of war are visible from the outside. The majority of service members who come home with serious injuries are forever changed. I am no exception. What would be asked from those I love most was unimaginable.

Once I was loaded in the medevac helicopter, my mind went blank; to this day I have not fully recovered my memory of the two weeks post-blast. When I finally came to,

> **Once I was loaded in the medevac helicopter, my mind went blank; to this day I have not fully recovered my memory of the two weeks post-blast.**

I was on more narcotic pain-killers than my body could handle. I had extreme hallucinations, so intense that at times I could not be left alone. The constant hum and buzz of the lifesaving equipment I was hooked to seemed very loud and abstract. I couldn't keep my mind from replaying the events of the explosion over and over. It was as if a twenty-four-hour news station were playing, so constant that at times I thought I was losing my mind.

The doctors kept saying I looked great. I knew I didn't. I was desperate for the truth—especially from someone who would not tell me how great I looked. Frustrated, I dragged myself to a deserted hallway to telephone a dear friend and found myself crying so hard I couldn't speak.

Out of my four-wall cocoon, I finally realized many service members were worse off than I, but that did not stop the stages of grieving. I saw hundreds of soldiers during my recovery who were in the same boat: passing through the rotating door of pain and healing, searching for our new normal, constantly longing for our former selves while struggling with the uncertainty of the war, which the comrades we left behind are still fighting.

Juanita was in a Humvee providing security for a convoy of supply trucks bringing ammunition and supplies to American troops in Iraq when a roadside bomb ripped through the side of the vehicle.

Many of the wounded warriors I have had the privilege to know at Walter Reed National Military Medical Center and over the years had such courage and fighting spirit that they gave me strength. Seeing what some of them had to overcome made fighting my own battles seem like a cakewalk. Our battle motto is "leave no man behind," but sometimes here at home our wounded feel they have to fight their personal war for recovery alone.

At last count, I have been rolled into the operating room twenty-seven different times and have had 102 medical procedures over a seven-year period. Like others who have been seriously wounded, I sometimes yearn for the person I once was. But I only have to look to the service member on my left or right to feel part of a very brave band of brothers and sisters.

So I was very honored to represent all of our country's wounded warriors when the Congressional Medal of Honor Society presented me with the Courageous Spirit Award in 2008. It can take years to recover, but the real heroes are those who made the ultimate sacrifice for our nation and the families they left behind.

The Congressional Medal of Honor Society presented Juanita Milligan with their Courageous Spirit Award in 2008.

A Daughter's Story

BY MATTIEMAE MILLIGAN

Let me start by saying that I love my mother very much. What I am about to reveal is truthful, although sometimes it is not pretty.

Being a teenager is hard enough, but my experience was also marked by the news that my mother's convoy had been hit by a roadside bomb in Iraq. When the family friend serving as one of our guardians woke me early one Saturday morning, I naturally assumed I was in trouble. As I walked up the stairs to our living room with my older brother, Scott, seventeen, an unspoken knowledge was in the air: Something was up. We met my younger brother, Sammy, twelve, in the hallway. As we made our way to the couch, both my guardians sat in front of us, their faces pale. When they began to tell us what had happened, my mind went numb.

Scott was moving into his life as an adult. Sammy had been diagnosed with autism when we were only toddlers. So when I heard the news about my mother, I knew that most of the responsibility of caring for our mother would fall on me. We had an enormous amount of help at the beginning. Getting things ready for my mother to come home required financial support as well as manual labor. I will be eternally grateful to every person who helped our family. But slowly that support faded, and even though I was just fourteen I became the "head" of our household. My new roles were nurse, cook, maid, counselor. Going to school every day caused me anxiety because I didn't know if my mother was safe at home, not from others but from herself. I wasn't old enough for a driver's license and made illegal trips in the car to various places, like the grocery store, at least twice a week. The weight of the responsibility I was given would make me feel resentful toward my mother. My definition of a normal life had been altered forever.

> When I heard the news about my mother, I knew that most of the responsibility of caring for our mother would fall on me.

The Long Wait for News

During the time between when we found out about the injury and when my mother returned to Walter Reed National Military Medical Center in Washington, DC, the only people able to communicate with the Army were my grandparents. The information we received about my mother was vague. We were unsure of how severe her injuries really were or when we would even be able to see her.

I traveled to visit my mother at Walter Reed several times after she came home. I will never forget the first time I saw her. She was lying there with a tangle of tubes connected to her. Bandages covered all of one side of her body. As we spoke to her, we realized it was going to be a long road back to her normal self. Now I know we were entirely too hopeful. Once, when she asked for some apple juice, I went out to the fridge to get her some. When I came back into her room, she

looked at me and got so excited. She had forgotten that I had been there just minutes before. We had to start our conversation over again. She couldn't understand why I began to cry a little when we were talking. Finally, I told her that I had been there for hours, and then she began to cry, too.

A Healthy Outlet

Coping was extremely difficult. As my mother healed, knowing which role I was playing, caretaker or daughter, involved a constant struggle between us. Each day I did what I had to do to get to the next day. I searched for activities that I could pursue given my new responsibilities. The only one that seemed to work was the sport of softball. I buried myself in it. Any spare time I could find, I would practice. I used this outlet to get away from my mother and my responsibilities. Eventually I would play in college.

Juanita's daughter, MattieMae, was just a teenager when she became her mother's chief caretaker and best friend. This photo was taken before Juanita was deployed to Iraq and subsequently injured.

If I have learned anything, it is that people do not change; life changes them. My mother will never be the woman who left home in 2004 to fight a war in a foreign country. For the longest time, I wrestled with this concept. Years passed before I could truly say that I understood and accepted that fact. Every once in a while, a glimmer of the woman I used to know comes back to life. I am grateful for every one of those instances, and I hope for them every day.

Many people call my mother a hero. But my heroes will forever be the men that saved her life on that fateful day, the men who risked their lives to save just one person. They will always have a special place in my heart.

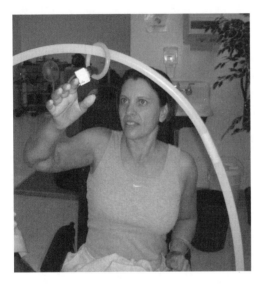

Juanita endured multiple surgeries and years of physical therapy to treat the severed nerves in her arm, side, and leg.

A RANGER LEADS THE WAY

"Those were my guys. I regarded them no differently than I would my children or my brothers."

"Never shall I fail my comrades." Those words are part of the creed of the 75th Ranger Regiment, one of the U.S. Army's most highly trained units, and the one given some of the most dangerous missions. Leroy Petry more than lived up to these words in the heat of battle in a remote village in Afghanistan.

★   ★   ★

Right before he began his senior year in high school in Santa Fe, New Mexico, Leroy Petry saw that he was headed toward a dead end. Because his parents worked such long hours to support the family—his father as a bus driver and his mother as a clerk at Walmart—he and his four brothers, all physical and competitive, spent a lot of time on their own. Leroy frequently got into fights in high school, trying to establish a reputation with his fists. He was a poor student, skipping school whenever he could. He got Ds and Fs and always raced to the mailbox when he knew his report card was about to arrive so that he'd get it before his parents did.

Realizing that he would soon graduate, Leroy took a look at his life, and he decided he didn't much like the person he was becoming.

· BORN, 1979, SANTA FE, NEW MEXICO
· ENLISTED IN U.S. ARMY, 1999
· RANK: SERGEANT FIRST CLASS
· UNIT: COMPANY D, 2ND BATTALION, 75TH RANGER REGIMENT
· SERVICE IN AFGHANISTAN, 2008
· REDEPLOYED TO AFGHANISTAN, 2011
· RECEIVED MEDAL OF HONOR, 2011

ROY PETRY

"If I want my future to be good," he realized, "I've got to start pushing myself."

Leroy changed schools to leave his old habits and reputation behind and start with a clean slate. He began studying and working for good grades, surprising himself with what he was able to accomplish when he concentrated. When he graduated, the local chamber of commerce awarded him its Bootstrap Award, given to the student who had worked hardest during the year to pull himself up from failure.

One reason Leroy worked to turn his life around was that he'd dreamed of joining the Army since he was a boy and knew that "the military doesn't take losers." Both his grandfathers had fought in World War II, an uncle had served in Vietnam, and a cousin had fought with the Rangers in Operation Desert Storm in 1991. The walls of his home were decorated with photos of these men in their uniforms. His family talked about their military achievements around the dinner table. Leroy wanted people to talk about him someday with the same respect.

In 1999, after trying college for a year to please his parents, Leroy, then twenty, enlisted in the Army. He joined the Rangers, which the Army calls its "premier direct action force," because he was so impressed with the slogan of this elite unit: Rangers lead the way.

Leroy enjoyed the hands-on activities of basic training, especially the days on the rifle range. He often stayed behind after the other recruits had finished shooting, continuing to practice his marksmanship. One day when he asked for more ammunition, his drill sergeant said to him, "You're going to be a Ranger, right?" Leroy replied that he was. The sergeant said, "Don't worry. You're going to be doing more shooting than you ever wanted to."

A few months after the 9/11 terrorist attacks on the World Trade Center and the Pentagon, Leroy's Ranger unit headed for Afghanistan. Images of the smoldering rubble of the Trade Center's Twin Towers were still fresh in his mind. "It was aimed at innocent civilians just going on with their everyday lives," Leroy says of the attack. "All these people who didn't ever find their family members . . . Knowing that we were going after the group that supported this mission was a big factor for me. It wasn't only revenge. It was a desire to stop this from ever happening again on American soil. If they want to shoot at us when we're over there, fine. But don't ever let this happen again to anybody back home."

Sergeant Leroy Petry on leave with his young son.

Special Mission

On May 26, 2008, Leroy, now a staff sergeant, was in the middle of his second tour in Afghanistan when his platoon was helicoptered to a remote area in the eastern part of the country to try to capture a "high-value target"—a Taliban leader thought to be hiding in a walled compound there. He knew that the mission had to be really important because the Rangers almost never undertook daylight actions. They preferred to operate in the dark, when night-vision goggles and other technology gave them an advantage. He knew that there would probably be a tough fight ahead because Taliban commanders were usually protected by well-armed, battle-hardened security teams.

As they approached the compound, Leroy made a mental map of the adobe-like buildings nestled in a desolate hilly area, noting the places where enemy fighters might be hiding. Almost as soon as they jumped out of their helicopter, the Rangers came under fire. Leroy was moving forward with his platoon leader when he saw another squad entering one of the smaller buildings in the compound. Because that squad's leader was inexperienced, Leroy yelled that he was going to help. The officer gave him a thumbs-up.

After clearing the building with the squad, Leroy ran toward a chicken coop in the courtyard with another Ranger, Private First Class Lucas Robinson, to make sure enemy forces weren't hiding there. What happened next remained engraved in his memory: "Out of the corner of my eye I see two Taliban stand up with AK-47s and start spraying from the hip. I was hit in the thigh. It felt like a sledgehammer pounding my leg. I put it out of my mind and kept moving. I saw Robinson get hit just below the left armpit."

"You Saved Us!"

The two men reached the shed and used it to shield themselves from enemy fire. Robinson had been saved from certain death by the side plate of his body armor. Leroy felt the blood from his leg wound trickling into his boot. He tossed a smoke grenade toward the Taliban as another Ranger, Sergeant Daniel Higgins, ran through the courtyard to support them. All three Americans were knocked down by a grenade, which sprayed them with shrapnel. Leroy had begun firing again when he saw another grenade land a few feet away from Robinson and Higgins. For a moment, time stopped: "I looked at the grenade and I looked at the guys behind me. Those were my guys—guys I was responsible for. I regarded them no differently than I would my children or my brothers."

> Leroy quickly picked the grenade up to throw it away from Robinson and Higgins.

Leroy quickly picked the grenade up to throw it around the corner of the shed away from Robinson and Higgins. But as he opened his hand to release it, the grenade exploded. Blood sprayed Leroy's protective glasses. When he took them off with his left hand, he saw that his right hand had been cleanly severed at the wrist. He studied the wound for a second, looking at the small pieces of shrapnel in the

Leroy Petry greets a young fan, showing him the marvel of his prosthetic hand.

stump and smelling the burning flesh. Then he refocused: He applied a tourniquet from his pack and called his commanding officer to report that three Rangers were down. As an afterthought, he added, "Oh, and my hand is gone."

Leroy switched his rifle to his left hand and continued firing. Other Rangers arrived to help, but he refused to be evacuated until the enemy fighters outside the shed were killed. Then he allowed himself to be taken to a casualty collection area, where medics worked on his arm. Noticing the blood spilling out of his boots, they cut off his pants and discovered that the bullet that hit him in the thigh had gone through both legs.

As the medics put Leroy on a stretcher and carried him to an evacuation helicopter, the other Americans firing from the rooftops of the buildings in the compound looked down and shouted encouragement. Sergeant Higgins rushed up and put a hand on Leroy's shoulder, yelling over the deafening noise of gunfire, "You saved us, man! You saved us!"

(Leroy's story continues on page 166.)

ARTIFICIAL LIMBS:
The Gifts of Science and Technology

Because of better body armor and advances in battlefield medicine, fewer soldiers are dying of their wounds than ever before. But that also means that more of them are coming home with very serious injuries—especially lost limbs.

Because of the IEDs (improvised explosive devices) planted along roads and hidden in cities that are the enemy's weapons of choice, more than seventeen hundred U.S. servicemen and women have lost limbs since the beginning of combat in Afghanistan in 2001. Recovery is physically and psychologically painful, but the chances of living a more normal life with these injuries have greatly improved as a result of advances in prosthetics, artificial arms and legs that function more and more like real limbs.

Leroy's prosthetic hand (above and opposite, bottom) can do many of the things a normal limb can do, including clutching a baseball and pledging allegiance. Artificial legs (opposite, top) now mimic a regular walking gait thanks to microchip gyroscopes implanted under the skin.

High-Tech Materials

Prosthetics are being made out of better materials than in the past—lighter, stronger plastics and carbon fiber. At one time artificial hands were merely hooks; now sensors the size of a grain of rice implanted in the patient's arm can detect nerve signals from undamaged muscles that allow a prosthetic hand to open and close and rotate 180 degrees. Artificial legs that once had to be "swung" from one step to another with difficulty now walk gracefully as a result of microchip gyroscopes implanted under the skin. Some amputees now have different artificial legs for different activities: cycling, hiking, dancing, martial arts, and ice-skating.

But while advances in prosthetics have meant a better quality of life for wounded servicemen and women, they don't answer the question many of these patients anxiously ask themselves when they return to civilian life: What will people see when they look at me?

Never Forget

During his nine months of care and rehabilitation at Brooke Army Medical Center in San Antonio, Texas, Leroy was fitted with a state-of-the-art artificial arm and hand. He immediately requested a small plaque made of plastic listing the names of the Rangers in his regiment who had been killed and had it bonded to his new prosthetic. "I see it every morning when I put it on and every afternoon when I take it off," he says. "That way I never lose sight of those who made the ultimate sacrifice."

Leroy planned to retire from the Army at the end of 2009 when his wounds were fully healed, but the day before he was scheduled to leave he decided to reenlist to work with injured Rangers. He was redeployed to Afghanistan, the only American soldier there serving with a prosthetic arm.

Leroy was awarded the Medal of Honor by President Barack Obama on July 12, 2011. As the president signed his citation, Leroy, noticing that he was left-handed, bent over and whispered, "Mr. President, now I'm left-handed, too. Any tips on how I can keep from smudging my handwriting?"

In 2011 President Barack Obama awarded fellow left-hander Leroy Petry the Medal of Honor "for conspicuous gallantry."

> Corporal Jason L. Dunham covered a grenade that was about to explode, putting his comrades before his own safety. A mother writes about what is left behind when a marine doesn't come home.

The Loss of a Son

BY DEB DUNHAM

"Medal of Honor Recipient Corporal Jason L. Dunham, United States Marine Corps, 2007, deceased." This is how history records the memory of this warrior and what people read when searching for information about this decorated marine. To us, our son represented so much more.

April 14, 2004, was the middle of school spring break and the Easter holiday for us in Scio, in the southern tier of New York State. My husband, Dan, was in bed, as were our two youngest children, Katie, eleven, and Kyle, fifteen. I was in the living room reading a novel, enjoying the few moments of peace and quiet every working mother craves.

The phone rang at 11:45 p.m. When the phone rings at that hour of the night, the sound is shrill and distinct; every nerve in your body jumps, and your gut hits the floor. Whoever is on the other end of the line probably does not have good news. I did a quick inventory: Katie and Kyle were asleep in their rooms; Justin, twenty-one, was living and working in Butler, Pennsylvania, just north of Pittsburgh, about three hours away; and Jason, twenty-two, our oldest son, was a marine deployed in

Deb Dunham hugs her oldest son, Jason, in an undated photograph,

Iraq. Instead of just picking up the phone, as I normally would have done, I found myself near the doorway of our bedroom calling my husband's name. He told me to answer.

On the other end of the line was a man calling from the marine base in Twentynine Palms, California. He said that Jason had been injured and was in critical condition. The information we received was brief and concise in the military way. It left us with countless questions and the dread that the worst could yet happen. But the phone call was and still is a blessing compared to a knock on the door, which is how the military normally contacts the family about a killed-in-combat death. We had the comfort of knowing that Jason was still alive.

Before he went overseas, or was deployed, several months earlier, Jason had spent his leave with us over the Christmas holiday. One evening during that visit, Dan and I sat curled together on the couch while all the kids were horsing around in one of the back bedrooms. Dan wanted to know how I felt about Jason being deployed. I told him I did not feel good about it. From his childhood, Jason had always looked out for the underdog. He had grown into a six-foot-one man, all muscle, and he could handle himself. Most of the time, when called on to settle a dispute, he would turn up the charm and was able to talk the situation toward an amicable result. But if called on to resolve something physically, he never hesitated. I knew that if something went wrong, Jason would be in the middle trying to protect those who needed help—and this was what made me uneasy.

That was exactly what had happened. Jason was serving as the squad leader of a marine platoon near the town of Al Karabilah, about seventy miles south of Baghdad, in Iraq. On the day we were told, he and his men had been called in because insurgents had attacked the battalion commander's convoy. Traffic was snarled, so they got out of their Humvee and began to search all vehicles for weapons. When they came to a white Land Rover, Jason ordered the driver to get out; instead, the driver jumped out of the vehicle, reaching for Jason's throat. Jason grabbed him, wrestling him to the ground, but the insurgent managed to drop a live grenade. Without hesitation, Jason covered the grenade with his helmet and body to shield his friends. It exploded, and some of the shrapnel lodged in his brain.

> **Without hesitation, Jason covered the grenade with his helmet and body to shield his friends.**

Jason was in a coma and not expected to recover when he was flown home to Bethesda Naval Hospital in Maryland. There, we were able to spend a brief but precious time with him. Dan sat on one side of his bed holding one of his hands; I sat on the other side holding his other. We linked our free hands over the bed. Medical staff, marines, and sailors, all there to honor a fellow warrior, filled the room. As Dan and I sat watching our child leave us, our hearts broke, never to mend in our lifetimes.

As excruciating as that moment was to live through, it was a second blessing that both Dan and I cherish to this day. We understand the gift that we had been given—having this brief time with Jason before he left us for his next journey. We had a chance to say good-bye.

Within three to four months' time, we learned that Jason had been

Jason Dunham, shown here in Iraq, was a twenty-two-year-old corporal when he covered an insurgent's grenade to save the lives of three other marines, an action for which he lost his life.

nominated for the Medal of Honor by the men he had served with. Dan had been in the Air Force and understood immediately what this honor meant. It took me a little longer. When you lose a child, you never "get over it." You find a "new normal," getting up each day to do the best you can.

When we finally learned that Jason was actually going to receive the Medal of Honor, we felt a host of emotions all at once: *pride* that our nation recognized the qualities we had always seen in our son as he grew up and that it was now validating his heroic act of selflessness with its highest award for valor; *sadness* that Jason was not here to accept this prestigious honor himself; and *awkwardness* in that people were congratulating *us* for *his* achievement. We hold fast to the fact Jason did the right thing. He probably would have been embarrassed by all the praise he received for doing what he would have perceived as his duty in saving the lives of his men.

> We try to honor Jason by helping others remember that our military, his brothers, continue to fight for and guard our freedoms.

The ceremonies that followed were a whirlwind—from the medal ceremony at the White House, to the induction into the Hall of Heroes in the Pentagon, to all the meetings with people who were incredibly kind to us. By the time we attended the closing ceremonies at the Marine Corps museum, it was all a blur. Since that day we have fielded thousands of invitations to attend military and civic events that want to honor Jason. We have learned to sort out the most important events to attend. But whenever possible, we try to honor Jason by helping others remember that our military, his brothers, continue to fight for and guard our freedoms.

Jason was the kid I constantly had to remind to take out the garbage, the one whose name I had to write in his clothes because he would leave them at his friends' homes. This is the son who would stop by my classroom to see how I was and if I had any extra food. This is the kid who, on leave, would gather up his three younger siblings from their classes, take them to lunch in the cafeteria, and charge "his" lunch to my account, knowing that it would be covered since I work in the same pre-K to 12 building my children attended. This is the boy who had no problem yelling down the hall in front of his friends, "Yo, Mama, I love you." I am so proud that he became part of a group that strives to protect and care for those who are not able to fend for themselves.

Every day, we feel a part of our hearts and lives are missing. The comfort in our loss is knowing that Jason chose to do the right thing. Three men are alive today because he acted boldly in the space of an instant to cover a grenade that might have killed them. They all have families today because of his actions. And who knows, God may have a plan that one of them or one of their children will do something great that benefits humanity, something that would not have been possible without Jason's courage.

Jason received the Medal of Honor for going above and beyond. For his father and me, he was merely doing something that day in Iraq that he had done in all the years that he was with us. What he did was who he was. We miss him dearly.

President George W. Bush presents Deb Dunham with the Medal of Honor awarded posthumously to her son Jason. To Deb's right is her husband, Dan. Partially hidden are their three children (from left), Kyle, Justin, and Katie.

HEROISM IN CIVILIAN LIFE

The Citizen Service Before Self Honors Award

Every single one of the Medal of Honor recipients you've just read about was someone who managed to find the inner resources to do something extraordinary in the chaos and crisis of war when others' lives were at stake.

But courage isn't restricted to the battlefield, as these military heroes know. "Everyday" citizens do heroic things all the time, either in a moment of bravery or a lifetime of service, and such acts of courage and self-sacrifice are part of our identity as Americans. These are people you might meet in your daily life, with one difference: They stepped up when others were stepping away, and they did the right thing when it would have been safer for them to do nothing at all.

Honoring Soldiers and Citizens Together

In 2007, Congress issued a proclamation naming May 25 as National Medal of Honor Day. The medal recipients decided that these unacknowledged Americans should be honored as well. And so they established, through the Medal of Honor Foundation, the Above and Beyond Citizen Honors Award (later renamed the Citizen Service Before Self Honors Award). They solicited nominations from all across the country for individuals who had risked their own lives or shown lasting dedication to the well-being of their fellow citizens. Three recipients of the Citizen Honors Award were honored on May 25, 2008, the second National Medal of Honor Day. (The medal is shown on the opposite page.)

Since then, the Citizens Honors awards ceremony has become an annual event, and many have been honored. Some—like the six teachers at Sandy Hook Elementary School in Connecticut who gave their lives to protect their students—have been recognized posthumously.

Other men and women recognized by the Citizen Service Before Self Honors Award survived their moments of heroism, among them several young people:

★ Seventeen-year-old Connor Stotts was swimming with friends near Oceanside, California, when a strong riptide swept them out to sea. Knowing that they might drown if he failed to act, Connor risked his own life to guide three of them to shore. Each time he got one of them to safety, he plunged back into the water to rescue another.

★ Jesse Shaffer III and his son, Jesse Shaffer IV, got into their boat during Hurricane Isaac when emergency vehicles couldn't navigate the flooded streets of their hometown of Braithwaite, Louisiana. Father and son began rescuing people trapped by the rising waters. During the next few hours, the Shaffers saved 120 people, even though their own home was destroyed.

★ Fourteen-year-old Marcos Ugarte ran to the aid of a seven-year-old boy trapped in the second story of a neighbor's burning house in Troutdale, Oregon. After Marcos's father and another man were overcome with smoke before they could rescue the boy, Marcos climbed onto the roof of the house, broke a window, and ran through the flames to bring the child out alive.

Paul Bucha, who was awarded the Medal of Honor for gallantry in Vietnam, spoke for all of the medal recipients when he said that these "ordinary persons, who reached within themselves and challenged destiny as they understood it to be," changed possibly tragic outcomes by their actions. Bucha believes that these citizens, like the men he fought with, "have the potential to change the world."

As you read about how the men and women you are about to meet put others before themselves, think about the challenge posed by Jack Jacobs, another Medal of Honor recipient: "Someday you, too, may be called upon to do something extraordinary. Will you do it?"

RICK RESCORLA

WARNINGS AND BRAVERY ON 9/11

"He could not have lived with himself unless he was the last man out of the building and there was no one else to save."

Rick Rescorla had predicted an attack against the World Trade Center long before 9/11. Despite being ill with cancer, he spent all the energy he had during his last years trying to convince the authorities that they had to do something. If only they had listened.

★　　★　　★

It's not that Rick craved attention. He was modest, reluctant to talk about his accomplishments. Even close friends were sometimes surprised to learn how crowded the hours of his life had been. He had emigrated to America from England and had been a highly decorated army officer in Vietnam. He had been a lawyer, although he no longer practiced, and a college professor, although he no longer taught. And despite how serious he seemed, his wife, Susan, later said of him, "People didn't realize that Rick was a song and dance man at heart."

What his friends did know was that in his "second career" as director of security for Morgan Stanley, the largest financial firm in New York City's World Trade Center, Rick had predicted a terrorist attack against

In Vietnam, Rick was known by the men in his platoon as "Hard Core" because of his bravery in battle.

that building years before September 11, 2001, and he believed that an attack against the Twin Towers would come from the air.

Rick's story began in the small English town of Hayle, Cornwall, where he was born in 1939. Rick fell in love with the United States as a boy while watching the U.S. 175th Infantry Regiment training for the 1944 D-Day invasion. He wanted someday to become a soldier and an American. He joined the British army after finishing high school and served in Cyprus and other hot spots. In 1960, he traveled to Africa, to present-day Zambia, in search of adventure and joined the Northern Rhodesia Police force.

As a result of his experiences as a soldier and soldier of fortune, Rick became a strong anti-Communist. In 1962 he returned to London, where he briefly worked in the metropolitan police force. The next year he emigrated to the United States, and although he wasn't a citizen, he joined the Army to fight against what he saw as the advance of Communism in Vietnam.

A Silver Star

After completing Officer Candidate School, Rick became a lieutenant in charge of a platoon in the U.S. 7th Cavalry Regiment. His unit participated in the historic Battle of Ia Drang in 1965, the first time U.S. forces met the North Vietnamese army head on.

Rick, whose men had given him the nickname "Hard Core" because of his mental as well as his physical toughness, played a key role in the two-day battle. Almost a hundred years earlier, the 7th Cavalry, commanded by George Armstrong Custer, was destroyed at Little Bighorn by Sioux warriors. At the beginning of the fight at Ia Drang, it seemed that the U.S. force, outnumbered by the North Vietnamese ten to one, might have a similar fate.

As darkness fell the first night, when his men feared that the enemy would overrun their position, Rick walked among them, reassuring them and singing songs from his native Cornwall in his rich baritone voice. When one frightened soldier asked him if they would make it through the next few hours, Rick replied, in a comment that would be remembered by the men who served with him long after the battle was over, that not only would they survive the night, but "when the sun comes up, we are going to kick some ass."

The Vietnamese forces suffered hundreds of casualties in the fight and were forced to withdraw. Although the Americans "won," they suffered huge losses: 79 dead and another 121 wounded. Rick received a Silver Star for his actions in the fight.

In Charge of Security

Rick now felt more than ever that he wanted to be an American. In 1967, he returned to the United States and left the army. He got a law degree, taught law for a time at the University of South Carolina, and became a citizen. But he still had a taste for action, and in 1985 he took a job

When the first plane hit the World Trade Center, Rick, head of security for the investment bank Morgan Stanley, used his bullhorn to direct his employees to get out of the building.

as head of security for the investment firm Dean Witter, headquartered in the World Trade Center in New York.

Rick was glad that Soviet Communism was headed toward collapse, but he believed that a new enemy was waiting in the wings—terrorism—and that the next war against America would be fought by small groups rather than large massed armies. "We're not going to go toe-to-toe on some battleground in the future," Rick told a television interviewer after taking his new job. "We'll see a kind of action we've never seen before."

More than a decade before the 9/11 attack, Rick invited Dan Hill, an old friend who had served with him in Vietnam and was now a security consultant, to come to New York to help him understand the ways in which the World Trade Center's Twin Towers might be open to attack. After examining the huge, unguarded parking garage of the building, Dan told Rick that if someone wanted to kill a lot of people, he could easily drive a truck filled with explosives into this basement, park it next to one of the columns supporting the structure, and detonate it by remote control after leaving the area.

The First Terror Attack

Even though Rick passed Dan's warnings on to New York City authorities and to his superiors at Dean Witter, no action was taken. But what Dan predicted was exactly what happened on February 26, 1993, when a small group of Islamic terrorists living in the United States and led by the so-called Blind Sheikh, Omar Abdul Rahman, detonated a massive truck bomb in the parking garage. The explosion didn't cause the North Tower of the World Trade Center to collapse into the South Tower, as the terrorists had hoped. But six people died in the attack, and hundreds were injured.

Even after this, Rick believed that the World Trade Center was still a terrorist target because of its symbolism as the largest structure in New York and one of the nerve centers of American capitalism. He and Dan believed that there would be another terrorist attack, but that it probably would come from the air rather than from the ground. The two men chartered a light plane and flew around the Twin Towers to figure out how an attack might be launched.

Firefighters carry a victim's remains from the ruins of the World Trade Center.

A rescue worker surveys the rubble from the collapse of the Twin Towers.

In 1997, Rick was diagnosed with an incurable cancer. While going through painful medical treatments to keep it under control, he continued to worry about the next terror strike. When Dean Witter was purchased by Morgan Stanley, he tried to convince its executives to move the headquarters from the World Trade Center. But the company had a long-term lease that would be expensive to break. Rick insisted that they at least install fireproof lights and smoke evacuators in the corridors. He had evacuation drills held every three months for the company's twenty-seven hundred employees, including the highest-paid executives. Rick timed every drill with a stopwatch. Some of the employees complained, but as one of them said later on, "I could go down those stairs with my eyes closed."

He had evacuation drills held every three months for the company's 2,700 employees.

A Prediction Comes True

Rick was in his office on the forty-fourth floor in the South Tower at the World Trade Center at 8:46 on the morning of 9/11 when the first hijacked plane hit the North Tower. While everyone else was frantically trying to figure out what had happened, Rick knew at once that it was an attack. He ordered Morgan Stanley employees on the thirty floors above him to get out of the building immediately.

As they were streaming down the stairwells, the second plane hit the South Tower at 9:03 a.m., causing it to lurch wildly and knocking Rick and many other people down. He picked himself up and, speaking into a bullhorn, urged everyone to remain calm and not trample each other. "We're good Americans," he said soothingly. "Walk slowly." He began to sing the Cornish songs he remembered from his youth, just as he had in the darkest moments of Vietnam.

Within a half hour, all but a handful of the twenty-seven hundred Morgan Stanley employees were out of the South Tower. As one executive left the building, he saw Rick going back up the staircase and told him to get out. Rick agreed that he would—but only after he made sure that none of the company's employees were still stranded in the floors above.

The South Tower collapsed a few minutes later. Rick's body was never found. Dan Hill, his friend of forty years, later said that Rick had died a soldier's death, just as he would have wanted: "He could not have lived with himself unless he was the last man out of the building and there was no one else to save."

In 2009, the Congressional Medal of Honor Society honored Rick with its Above and Beyond Citizen Honors Award. The words at the ceremony, spoken by Medal of Honor recipient Paul Bucha, summarized Rick's life: "Inside all of us a hero lives. For some it will rise up and show itself through an extraordinary act of courage on the battlefields of their everyday lives."

Some of the details of Rick Rescorla's life come from his biography, *Heart of a Soldier,* by James B. Stewart (Simon & Schuster, 2002).

Rick's children, Trevor and Kim, receive the Medal of Honor Society's Above and Beyond Citizen Honors Award on Rick's behalf from medal recipients Paul Bucha (left) and Robert Howard.

SURPRISE ATTACK: *The Events of 9/11*

On the morning of September 11, 2001, four U.S. airliners took off from airports in Boston, Newark, and Washington, D.C., headed for the West Coast. They never made it. About thirty minutes into the air they were hijacked by Islamic terrorists, who killed all the crew members using knives and box cutters they smuggled on board. The terrorists then took control of the jets. There were four or five terrorists on board each airliner, and one on each with enough flight training to serve as pilot.

When American Airlines Flight 11 smashed into the North Tower of New York City's World Trade Center, it first seemed that a terrible accident had taken place. But as a horrified nation watched on television, a second plane, United Flight 175, flew directly into the World Trade Center's South Tower, and it was clear that the crashes were no accident. In the intense fires that followed, both towers collapsed, killing nearly three thousand people, including hundreds of New York City firemen, policemen, and other first responders. The unimaginable had happened: America had been attacked on its own soil.

The skyline of lower Manhattan in New York shows the Twin Towers before terrorists destroyed them on September 11, 2001, killing almost three thousand people.

Two More Plane Crashes

At about the same time, American Flight 77 slammed into the Pentagon, killing sixty-four people on board and 125 Defense Department employees and members of the U.S. military. A fourth airliner, United Flight 93, was headed toward the White House or the U.S. Capitol Building but never reached its target: Cell phone calls from the passengers to airline workers and loved ones sketched a picture of the passengers' brave decision to fight back against the hijackers. One yelled, "Let's roll!" as they started their counterattack, and it became our nation's battle cry. As a result of the passengers' efforts, United Flight 93 crashed in a Pennsylvania field, killing all forty-four on board, rather than into a government building in Washington.

The Pentagon in Arlington, Virginia, suffered extensive damage in the 9/11 attacks, and 184 people were killed.

Of the nineteen terrorist hijackers, fifteen were Saudis, two were from the United Arab Emirates, one was from Egypt, and one was from Lebanon. They were all well educated, spoke English, and had spent time living in Western countries, including the United States.

Osama bin Laden, head of the terror organization al-Qaeda, admitted that he had sent these men to attack America mainly because of its support of Israel and the troops the United States maintained in Middle Eastern countries.

The mastermind behind the 9/11 attacks was Osama bin Laden, head of the terror group al-Qaeda. He was killed in Pakistan by a team of U.S. Navy SEALs in 2011.

JENCIE FAGAN

A TEACHER'S LESSON IN COURAGE

"If you see something happening that isn't right, you do something."

On the snowy morning of March 14, 2006, physical education teacher Jencie Fagan was in the school gym putting up a volleyball net for her first-period class at the Edward L. Pine Middle School in Reno, Nevada. Jencie was one of the most popular members of the school's faculty. She was known for her enthusiasm, her high expectations, and her willingness to become personally involved with her students—the sort of teacher who would assign her class to run laps around the school track, then jog with the kids in the back who were having trouble keeping up, urging them on to do their best.

With a teenage child of her own, Jencie understood the social and personal conflicts that students sometimes have to deal with. "Our kids here are middle school children with all the issues kids their age have," she says. "But they have beautiful hearts."

For Jencie that snowy morning, seeing the beauty of fourteen-year-old James Newman's heart would take an enormous act of courage.

★   ★   ★

James was one of the loners at Edward L. Pine. School was a real struggle for him, and he had a dark feeling that no one—not his schoolmates or his parents—cared enough about him. His anger and confusion had come to a boil a few days earlier when he watched an online video of the 1999 Columbine High School shootings in Colorado, in which two deranged students murdered twelve of their classmates and a teacher and wounded twenty-four others. Perversely inspired by the actions of the Columbine students, James had put his parents' .38 caliber pistol in his backpack before he left for school that morning, went into a bathroom to remove it when he arrived, and came out ready to shoot.

One of his friends who passed James in the hall pleaded with him to put the gun away. James told the boy to run for his life. Then he opened fire randomly, hitting one eighth-grade student in the arm and another in the leg.

Jencie, busy in the gym, heard three sharp sounds, as if someone had slammed some books down on the floor. Fearing something more serious, she sprinted to the cafeteria next door, which seemed to be where the noises were coming from. In the hallway, she saw panicked students running in all directions and staff members in the hallways yelling, "Code red! Code red!" She saw one teacher hurry into her office and lock the door behind her. Several students seemed frozen with fear; Jencie ordered them into her office.

> **In the hallway, she saw panicked students running in all directions and staff members in the hallways yelling, "Code red! Code red!"**

For one young, frightened observer, Jencie's appearance on the scene was anything but surprising. Kendra Hess, a student who was still hiding behind a pillar in the cafeteria, terrified that she'd be killed by the gunman, felt a ray of hope when she saw Jencie. "Yes!" she thought to herself. "If anybody here can save me, Mrs. Fagan will."

Seeing James holding the gun, ready to fire again, Jencie walked up to him and began talking to him in a soft voice. She kept telling him that he was not a killer and that he would be all right. Worried that if some other student accidentally walked into the cafeteria, he'd turn and shoot, she stood in front of James so that he would have to look directly at her and so that the bullet would hit her if he did pull the trigger.

"You Never Quit"

Jencie felt sympathy for James even as she was determined to keep him from hurting anyone else. In dealing with troubled teens like him, she always remembered the difficulties she had experienced when she was their age. One of six kids brought up by a single mother in a small town in Alabama, she had sometimes felt disadvantaged in comparison to more "normal" families. But her mother, who worked long hours to keep the household going, wouldn't tolerate self-pity. "When things got difficult, Mom didn't give up," Jencie remembers. "She just pushed harder. She taught us that you never quit."

This determination not to run away from problems was what made Jencie come forward that morning when everyone else was trying to save themselves. Standing close to James and forcing him to make eye contact by looking directly at his face, she talked in a soothing tone, repeatedly asking him to set the pistol on the floor. He looked disoriented and hesitated for a long time, but finally he dropped the gun. Jencie immediately grabbed him and hugged him tightly, both to restrain and reassure him. "I'm here," she whispered to him. "I'm not going anywhere." She continued to hold him until the police arrived.

Edward L. Pine Middle School was put on lockdown for the rest of the day. The two wounded students were treated at a local hospital and released that afternoon. James was arrested. He was later tried as a minor and convicted of two counts of battery with a deadly weapon.

> **Standing close to James and forcing him to make eye contact by looking directly at his face, she talked in a soothing tone, repeatedly asking him to set the pistol on the floor.**

When she was asked why she had put herself in harm's way, Jencie talked about her mother: "Mom raised us to think that if you see something happening that isn't right, you do something. You don't look for someone else to handle it. I'm a teacher, a mom, a human being. These are our children. There's no way I'm having to call a parent after something has happened and tell them I didn't protect their kid."

Two years later, on March 25, 2008, the Congressional Medal of Honor Society presented Jencie Fagan with its Above and Beyond Citizen Honors Award in a ceremony at Arlington National Cemetery attended by thirty-four Medal of Honor recipients. As former U.S. secretary of state Colin Powell put the ribbon around her neck, one of these recipients, Paul Bucha, reminded the large audience that what Jencie had done on that awful day in Nevada showed that "every one of us has the capacity for courage and heroism."

In recognition of teacher Jencie Fagan's selfless bravery in risking her life to save her students, General Colin Powell presented her with the Congressional Medal of Honor Society's Above and Beyond Citizen Honors Award in 2008.

In a life-or-death situation, when the lives of a soldier's comrades are on the line, nothing in the past matters as much as acting in the moment. Medal of Honor recipient Allen Lynch reflects on the insults and mistreatments he once suffered growing up, and how combat taught him what was most important in the end.

On Being Bullied and Learning Self-Respect

BY ALLEN LYNCH

We were pinned down and under intense enemy fire. One of our fighter jets flew over our heads so low that we could count the rivets on its wings. It released a bomb that I was sure would hit us. It exploded in a flash of fire and scorching heat about one hundred feet from us. We were still alive! We had just gone through several artillery barrages, being strafed and bombed; a piece of shrapnel even landed on my leg, and I had a bloody nose from the explosion. To make matters worse, the enemy was so close that we could hear them talking. I was afraid. But then I was used to being afraid.

I was bullied from grade school through high school. It started in the fourth grade. Three boys transferred into my school, and for the next four years they bullied me mercilessly. They did the usual things that kids still do today—tripping me as I walked down the hall, knocking my books from my hand, even urinating in my gym shoes. They called me at home and told me what was going to happen to me the next day. I was beaten up several times. Strangely, fighting back never entered my mind. All I had to do was get a couple of good licks in each time and I could have ended it, but I was overcome with paralyzing fear. I felt less than worthless. I withdrew into myself and trusted no one. Things deteriorated both at school and at home. My parents were disappointed in me because of my poor grades and lack of friends. They wanted me to enjoy school, but all I desperately wanted was to be left alone.

When his company was ambushed in a firefight in Vietnam in December 1967 and forced to withdraw, Allen Lynch stayed with his comrades and then carried each of the wounded men through heavy fire to safety.

Our family moved in 1960 after I graduated from junior high school. I was moving away from the bullies and going to a school where no one knew me. What I didn't know was that no matter where you go, there *you* are. Change must come from within.

Things started well. I actually began making friends. But the first time I was confronted, the boy I thought I left behind reappeared. Bullies are in every school, and this one was no different. I was the new kid, and the rules of the playground dictated that I be challenged. One day at lunchtime, I sat at the wrong table and a kid told me to move. I thought, *This is my chance; this time I won't back down.* I stood up, and all the old fears flooded over me. I felt totally defeated. I stopped going to school events. My grades suffered; I failed math and had to go to summer school twice. The bullying was less threatening than before, but my old fears of rejection and lack of self-esteem were as strong as ever. More than anything, it was my self-doubt that hindered me. That isn't to say I didn't have friends; I did. But my friends were outsiders like me. The girls I dated were few and far between. I even had a few fights and didn't do too badly, but I just didn't fit in.

In 1964, I graduated from high school. But being a poor student, lacking confidence and a sense of purpose, I had limited choices. I was sure I would be drafted eventually, so I enlisted in the Army. Our drill sergeant taught us to be soldiers: to meet tough standards, to rely on each other, and to work together as a team—our lives would depend on it. As we succeeded in becoming soldiers, I became more confident in my abilities. I learned to run and chant cadence as we marched, to shoot and hit the target (I qualified as expert). I learned to work with others to achieve goals; the Army calls it "accomplish the mission." I learned the four life-saving steps: Stop the bleeding, protect the wound, clear the airway, and treat for shock. Knowing these would help me to save lives in December 1967. My confidence was growing, but I still had a very long way to go.

During high school, rather than go to study hall I often went to the library. When my homework was done, I read history; I think I read every history book in the library. After I was in basic training for four weeks, I was asked if I wanted to go to Officer Candidate School. If I could make it through the six months of training, I'd become an officer. I thought that finally I could do something to make my parents proud of me. But I again found that no matter where you go, there you are. I had grown and gained confidence, but not enough. I took the long hours and constant pressure by our tactical officers personally. After four weeks, I dropped out. I had failed again! But the Army taught me something: I failed, but I learned that I could endure long hours of hard physical and mental work. I learned to study like I never did before. And I learned I could fail but didn't have to give up.

> **I was part of something bigger than myself and felt I was part of the team.**

I was soon transferred to Germany. A year later I volunteered for Vietnam. I served in combat with the D Company, 1/12 Cavalry, 1st Cavalry Division. By December 1967, I had been in combat for six months. I'd been in firefights, rocketed and mortared, gone on ambushes, and served in observation posts. I was part of something bigger than myself and felt I was part of the team. We relied on each other, and we trusted each other with our lives. During those six months, I lost my best friend to friendly fire. I saw the dead on both sides; I can still see them. The dead soldiers I helped to load onto helicopters still haunt me. But in all the hardship of combat, I started to find myself.

On December 15, we were on a mission to relieve one of our companies that had been ambushed the day before. As we moved to help them we, too, were ambushed. It seemed like everyone started firing at the same time. It was a nightmare of noise with machine guns, rifle fire, hand grenades exploding, and men yelling all around. I followed my lieutenant as he ran to the front to assess the situation. I was his radioman; it was my job to stay with him so we could inform headquarters about what was happening.

The enemy fire was intense, and there were wounded who needed help. I had to act; there was no time for fear. I asked the lieutenant if I could drop my radio and go out to get the men who were down. I saw a trench and started moving them there. I don't remember how I did it. I was too busy. All I know was that my training and the core values taught

As Allen Lynch learned in Vietnam, American soldiers care for their wounded even in the heat of battle under enemy fire. No one is left behind.

to me by my parents, family, and military leaders kicked in. In the end, I had gotten the wounded to a safer place. I remembered my lifesaving steps as I cared for their wounds. Those steps had become such a part of me that I didn't have to even think about them; I just did them.

As we lay pinned down in the trench fighting for our lives, my only thoughts were that I couldn't let down the men who counted on me to get them out. I was afraid, but not for myself. Once, as our company was trying to rescue us, they told me to leave the men; we'd get them later. But I couldn't do it; they were my responsibility, and we don't leave our wounded.

After the fighter jet dropped napalm and another jet strafed close to our position, there was dead silence. It was now or never. I checked the surrounding area for the enemy and started looking for a safer location. Then I carried the wounded one by one from our position to friendly lines.

I didn't realize it then, but from that day on I stopped being afraid of what others thought of me. I no longer cared if they liked me or not. For the first time in my life, I was my own person, no longer needing or seeking the approval of others. I still had to grow, for we never lose the need to grow, to change, to become better people, but I was on my way.

When I received the Medal of Honor, I had no idea how much it was going to change my life. The medal stands for the best of America— selfless service, courage, and sacrifice. The Army taught me duty, honor, and service. The medal put me in a position to continue serving, which I do by sharing my story with disadvantaged kids, parents, and teachers. Through the Allen J. Lynch Medal of Honor Veterans Foundation, we help veterans of all eras who need assistance.

Most of all, I learned never to lose faith in God. If we allow it, every negative circumstance in life can be used as an occasion to grow and to help other people. When I acted, it was the result of all those who influenced me throughout my life—my parents, grandparents, family, drill sergeant, and, in a sense, even those who bullied me. In the end, I am the sum total of all my life experiences, the good ones and the bad ones. All of them made me who I am today.

JORDY COX

HEALING THE WORLD,
ONE PATIENT AT A TIME

"You do what your heart tells you to do."

A volunteer with a relief organization called Doctors Without Borders, Dr. Jordy Cox went to the Democratic Republic of the Congo in 2008 to save lives, but on his first day at work there in the middle of a vicious civil war, he thought he might lose his own.

★   ★   ★

Previously Jordy had worked as a trauma surgeon in Africa's Ivory Coast during its first civil war. There, treating people whose arms had been hacked off by machetes, he thought he would never again witness such horrifying violence. But that bloodshed couldn't compare to what he saw in Congo, where both sides tortured and killed prisoners and civilians.

The situation was so dangerous on the day Jordy arrived in Rutshuru, a town in the eastern part of Congo, that the United Nations peacekeeping force evacuated the entire medical staff of the hospital. He and another surgeon with Doctors Without Borders volunteered to stay behind and treat the injured by themselves.

Dozens of people maimed by the battle raging in the streets outside the hospital streamed into the operating room during Jordy's first days at work. Most were civilians caught in the crossfire of the warring forces. But one was an officer in the Congolese army, carried into the hospital with a gunshot wound in the chest. Jordy immediately operated, removing a bullet lodged dangerously close to the man's heart. A few hours later, as the officer was in recovery and Jordy was working on other patients, a rebel commander walked in, two men carrying machine guns on either side of him. He demanded to know where the Congolese officer was. When Jordy refused to tell him, the rebel pulled out a pistol and said, "If you don't take me to see him, I will put this gun in your mouth and kill you." Somehow, Jordy talked the rebel out of killing either him or the wounded officer. Then he went back to the operating table.

> **The rebel commander demanded to know where the Congolese officer was. When Jordy refused to tell him, the rebel pulled out a pistol and said, "If you don't take me to see him, I will kill you."**

For the next month, Jordy didn't leave the hospital. "There was fighting raging in the streets right around us," he recalls. "Tanks were firing and bombs falling literally right outside." He did one operation after another on people mutilated by the war. "You sleep when you can," he recalls of his daily routine. "You eat when you can. You just deal."

Citizen of the World

Before going to Congo, Jordy was a surgeon at the Maricopa Medical Center in Phoenix, Arizona. But it was on his trips to the underdeveloped world that Jordy felt most needed. "If I'm going to be given the choice between an assignment that doesn't have danger and one that does," he says, "I'm going to sign up for the dangerous one."

One especially dangerous assignment he volunteered for was in Pakistan, a place where the sudden violence of the suicide bomber is the norm. "I remember the sound of the explosion," Jordy says of one suicide bombing that took place near where he was treating patients. "There is an evil that goes along with that noise."

A 7.2-magnitude earthquake devastated Haiti on January 12, 2010. Dr. Jordy Cox was on a plane to the capital, Port-au-Prince, the next afternoon. Over the next ten days, he worked with a surgical team in a makeshift operating room in a tent because all the hospitals in the city had been destroyed.

Jordy has wanted to work in such remote and threatening places not only because of sympathy for the victims of conflict there—people who otherwise wouldn't be able to get emergency medical treatment—but also because he has always felt that he was a citizen of the world. He was born in 1972 near Barcelona to an English father and Swiss mother. He grew up speaking English, Spanish, and French. When he was a boy he wanted to be a movie stuntman. Later he wanted to be a veterinarian. And finally he decided that he would become a doctor.

But a normal practice as a general practitioner wasn't what Jordy had in mind. Instead, he wanted to help people who had experienced extreme injuries, and after finishing medical school in Spain, he came to the United States for advanced training in trauma surgery. He heard that Doctors Without Borders was looking for what it called "conflict surgeons" to work in areas troubled by civil unrest and natural disaster, and immediately signed up. His wife, Heidi, a pediatric surgeon who once was in the U.S. Air Force, also volunteers for Doctors Without Borders and has provided medical treatment in Nigeria and other global hot spots.

Haiti

Jordy has close ties to his patients in the United States, but he is always on the alert for the next international disaster. He had just gotten home from work in Arizona on the evening of January 12, 2010, when he heard on a Phoenix radio station that a massive earthquake had hit Haiti. "I knew right away they'd be needing help," he remembers. A call came from Doctors Without Borders a couple of hours later. The next morning Jordy spoke with the three surgeons he worked with. All of them had children and couldn't leave to go to Haiti, but they told Jordy they would fill in for him during his trip as their way of also helping the disaster victims.

Jordy was on a plane to Haiti early that afternoon. But he was not prepared for what he saw when he arrived in the Haitian capital of Port-au-Prince. In the civil wars he had seen in the Ivory Coast and Congo, buildings were often riddled by bullets but still standing. In Port-au-Prince the earthquake had leveled them all. Injured people were lying in the streets; search-and-rescue teams in bright orange vests were pulling bodies out of the rubble; the smell of death was in the air. One of the city's main hospitals had been destroyed. Jordy and the other surgeons established a new "operating room" in a parking lot by hanging sheets around a raised wooden platform.

Many of the patients' arms and legs had been mangled by falling concrete when the powerful quake first struck. Jordy spent his first days amputating limbs to save lives. He and the rest of the team did approximately forty major operations a day. In each of the cases he worked on, he felt the personal tragedy. "One of the reasons you become a surgeon and put yourself in this type of environment is because you care," he says. But in addition to feeling pity for the victims of the disaster, he was also aware of their quiet bravery. One case that he would never forget involved two young girls, three and seven years old, and a woman with them. Each of the girls had to have a leg amputated. The woman had suffered some bone fractures but was otherwise all right and more worried about the children than herself. "I assumed that she was their mother," Jordy recalls. "But it turned out that she had never met them until the earthquake hit and had been taking care of them since."

In the first ten days after the disaster, the surgical team Jordy was part of saw more than a thousand badly injured patients. They lost only eleven.

I Was Just Doing My Job

On March 25, 2010, the Congressional Medal of Honor Society awarded Dr. Jordy Cox its Citizen Service Before Self Honors Award (formerly known as the Above and Beyond Citizen Honors Award) in a ceremony at Arlington National Cemetery. Afterward, Jordy talked to some of the Medal of Honor recipients. "They all had done things for their country they never thought they could do, amazing things," he says. "But when I talked to them about it, they all said to me, 'I was just doing my job.' In a way, that's what I think about myself. I was just doing my job. You do what your heart tells you. That's what you're supposed to do."

On March 25, 2010, the Congressional Medal of Honor Society awarded Jordy its Citizen Service Before Self Honors Award for his work with Doctors Without Borders all over the world.

DOCTORS WITHOUT BORDERS

Doctors Without Borders is the American branch of the French organization Médecins Sans Frontières (MSF), which was started in 1971 when a small group of French doctors came to the aid of the Igbo people of Biafra, a part of southeastern Nigeria. Biafra was suffering brutal attacks by the Nigerian army in revenge for its attempts to declare independence. The International Red Cross didn't step in, saying the war was an "internal matter" for Nigeria to handle. So the doctors formed Médecins Sans Frontières and vowed to address the medical needs of people in crisis situations despite the politics of their countries.

Today Médecins Sans Frontières sends some 28,000 volunteers—doctors, nurses, communicable-disease specialists, and water and sanitation engineers—to more than sixty countries around the world. Its mission is to respond rapidly to medical emergencies caused by civil wars, epidemics of diseases such as AIDS and the Ebola virus, and natural catastrophes such as earthquakes and floods, and also to make sure that the world knows that these tragedies are taking place.

Dedication and Sacrifice

MSF volunteers have been killed by land mines, armed attacks, and the diseases they were trying to combat. They have been kidnapped. During the 1994 Rwandan genocide, when upward of one million people were slaughtered in tribal conflicts, more than a hundred local MFS volunteers lost their lives.

But the organization continues to grow. MSF provides doctors for powerless people desperate for medical care and speaks out about health crises even when governments sometimes deny they are happening. In 1997, Médecins Sans Frontières received the Nobel Peace Prize. In accepting the award, the organization's president, Dr. James Orbinski, said, "We are not sure that words can save lives, but we are sure that silence can kill."

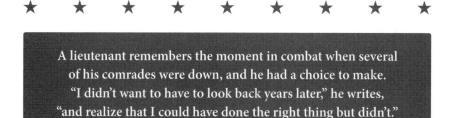

★ ★ ★ ★ ★ ★ ★ ★ ★

A lieutenant remembers the moment in combat when several
of his comrades were down, and he had a choice to make.
"I didn't want to have to look back years later," he writes,
"and realize that I could have done the right thing but didn't."

★ ★ ★ ★ ★ ★ ★ ★ ★

On Serving Others Before Self

BY JACK JACOBS

In March 1968, I was an army infantry lieutenant and, along with three other Americans, an adviser to a South Vietnamese infantry battalion. We accompanied them on every military operation. We lived together, ate together, and fought together, and we felt that we were as much a part of the Vietnamese army as we were part of the U.S. Army.

Being in Vietnam in 1968 meant that we were in combat every single day for months on end. On March 9, my noncommissioned officer (NCO), Staff Sergeant Ray Ramirez, and I were with the lead company of the battalion when we were ambushed in the open by about 250 enemy soldiers. Many of our troops were killed immediately, and many more, including Ramirez and myself, were hurt in the initial seconds of the battle.

I was wounded in the head, blood gushing from it alarmingly. Because there was a small piece of shrapnel stuck in my eye, I couldn't see anything out of it. I was focused on only one thing: the tiny world of my fellow warriors with whom I spent all of my time. It didn't matter

that they were Vietnamese and I was an American. They were my comrades. I could hear bullets and shrapnel whizzing around continuously, hitting the ground, smacking sickeningly into my friends just a few feet away.

Even the bravest people are scared in combat, but being badly hurt makes you even more afraid. At first there's a feeling of helplessness as you see your friends killed and wounded. But soon—and most people with combat experience will tell you the same thing—you are calmed by the understanding that you and your comrades are related: brothers, really, through service and sacrifice. It's true that we fight for our country, but when the chips are down, we really fight for each other.

In the midst of all this chaos, I thought of the teaching of a first-century Hebrew scholar named Hillel. Almost two thousand years ago he

TOP: U.S. Army lieutenant Jack Jacobs enjoys a lighthearted moment (top) on the American base in Vietnam in 1967.

LEFT: In 1968 Jack Jacobs, with a Vietnamese soldier, was serving as an adviser to a battalion of the Army of the Republic of South Vietnam.

asked these questions: If not you, who? And if not now, when?

What that meant to me at that moment was that somebody had to act or all of my friends would be killed. And if I didn't do it, who could? I decided that even though I was hurt, I was the only person who was capable of action, and I wasn't going to let the chance pass by. I didn't want to have to look back years later and realize that I could have done the right thing but didn't.

Despite the pain in my head and all the blood, I dragged about two dozen of my friends, who were out in the open being hit with rifle and machine-gun fire, to a safer area nearby that had a few trees to stop some of the bullets. After that, I

Jack saved thirteen members of his unit after it was ambushed on March 9, 1968. In addition to the Medal of Honor, Jack received two Silver Stars, three Bronze Stars, and two Purple Hearts.

collapsed from loss of blood and was evacuated to a field hospital. In the end, the lives of one U.S. adviser and thirteen allied soldiers were saved, and I am grateful that I did my best for them.

Today, we live in a very complex world, and most people are motivated to act only for themselves. But think about this: None of us would be here if it weren't for the selfless sacrifice of the people who came before us—Washington's troops, who braved the awful winter at Valley Forge and then defeated the British to give to us the United States of America; the heroes who defeated the Axis during the Second World War and brought a generation of peace to the world; the brave men and women who, after the attacks of September 11, 2001, volunteered to fight terrorism and who are still serving today.

But heroism isn't confined to the battlefield. There are Americans performing acts of valor every day, when they volunteer to help their fellow citizens, when they stand up to unfairness, when they battle bullies. In my experience, physical courage is relatively easy, but it's moral courage that is real heroism. When a natural disaster occurs, it's easy to ignore it, but the person with genuine courage tries to help out. When a thoughtless person makes fun of someone who can't defend himself or herself, it takes courage to set the record straight. When we encounter lies, cheating, and stealing, all of which make our communities poorer, it takes courage to report it. Choosing to do the right thing will change your life and those of your friends for the better and forever.

And this is the lesson I learned in combat, when the world was collapsing around me, when I thought I wouldn't survive to see the next sunrise: There is no limit to what we can accomplish if we take care of each other. The next time you have the choice to do something only for yourself, or to do something for your community instead, keep in mind something Benjamin Franklin once said: "We must all hang together, or assuredly we shall all hang separately." In other words, we're all in this together.

AFTERWORD

THE CONSEQUENCES OF WAR

As Tibor Rubin, recipient of the Medal of Honor for his actions during the Korean War, came down a hill following a battle in which he had single-handedly held off dozens of the enemy, he was glad to be alive, but he was also aware of what he had just done. "I killed the enemy, but I've killed somebody's father, brother, uncle . . . " It was a moment of personal triumph, but the conclusion Rubin drew was one that all soldiers would agree with: "War is hell."

Soldiers fight for their country, and most of all they fight for each other. They do what they have been trained to do. Most soldiers hate war. They see buddies maimed or killed. Day after day, they endure uncertainty, almost unbearable stress, and risk. They leave families behind to deal with the crises of daily life on their own. Some soldiers return home with disabling injuries or haunting memories that remain with them for years or even a lifetime. When Geno Merli, another recipient of the Medal of Honor, was asked about the action for which he was recognized—killing fifty-two German soldiers in a twelve-hour-long battle in Belgium near the end of World War II—he said that the first thing he did when the fighting ended was go to a nearby chapel and pray for the buddies he had lost and the enemy soldiers he had been forced to kill.

War is hell, too, for civilians—the men, women, and children who inevitably get caught in the cross fire. There has never been a war in modern times that has spared these people from its terrible consequences. They are victims, sometimes political pawns. They mourn fathers and mothers, sons and daughters, and others who went to war, never to come home. They are frequently forced out of their homes and left to live in squalid conditions, going hungry, and sometimes suffering unspeakable atrocities. They are killed in staggering numbers. The economic impact of bombed cities and destroyed industries is huge, and it affects future generations. During World War II, somewhere between sixty million and eighty-five million civilians lost their lives either by direct or indirect effects of the war—much more than the military losses.

Soldiers understand the costs of war, both for civilians and for those on the battlefield. John Hawk was a recipient of the Medal of Honor in World War II and a schoolteacher for more than thirty years afterward. He told the story about a student who asked him out of the blue one day, "Mr. Hawk, what's it like to kill somebody?" Hawk recalled: "That question is a kick in the gut. You have to have an honest answer for your students because they have complete faith in you. I tried to explain that the worst thing that can happen to a human being is to have to take the life of another human being. It's something you will never, ever forget." He told the student that there was only one reason soldiers were able to do this terrible thing: "That reason is you. Think about that on Veterans Day."

THE MEDAL OF HONOR

★ ★ ★ ★ ★

THEN AND NOW

The Medal of Honor was created by Congress in 1861 and signed into law by President Abraham Lincoln as the bloody Civil War was just beginning. It is the nation's highest military honor, standing for courage and sacrifice.

Recipients of the medal have been privates and seamen, admirals and generals, teachers, businessmen, laborers, and professionals, immigrants, and members of minorities. They have come from every walk of American life.

One recipient in 1869 was a Pawnee army scout in the Indian Wars named Co-Rux-Te-Cod-Ish ("Mad Bear"). The first black serviceman to perform an action for which the medal was awarded was William Carney, a sergeant in the all-black 54th Massachusetts Infantry Regiment. William saved the American flag from capture during the regiment's assault on Fort Wagner despite being wounded several times. The only woman ever to receive the medal was Dr. Mary Walker, who served as a civilian surgeon during the Civil War. One American, later to become president, Theodore Roosevelt, was awarded the medal for his actions on San Juan Hill during the Spanish-American War, as was his son, Theodore Roosevelt Jr., for his actions during the D-Day landings in World War II.

What most of the medal recipients have in common is the belief that they didn't "win" the honor for themselves. Instead, they merely hold it in trust for their comrades who never came home and as inspiration for those who will have to defend the country in the future.

Here are a few of the reasons that the Medal of Honor is distinctive:

★ Of an estimated forty million men and women who have served in the United States military over the last 150 years, fewer than thirty-five hundred have received the medal. Nearly half of those were in the Civil War.

★ It is the only medal normally presented by the president of the United States.

★ Its recipients are the only individuals the president salutes as a matter of custom. Harry Truman, who awarded more Medals of Honor during his time in office (1945–53) than any other U.S. president, often said, "I would rather have this medal around my neck than be president of the United States."

★ In the great military struggles that have defined modern America—World War II, Korea, Vietnam, and now the conflicts in Afghanistan and Iraq—more than 60 percent of all medals have been awarded posthumously.

★　★　★

World War I

It was the United States' entry into World War I in 1917 that made much of the American public aware of the Medal of Honor for the first time. The development of moving-picture cameras meant that this was the first war that was seen at home even as it was happening. Newsreels of the battlefronts appeared on silent-movie screens across the country, and human-interest stories about American fighting men pumped up the circulation of big-city newspapers. For the first time, Medal of Honor recipients became celebrities.

The most famous of them was a Tennessee farmer named Alvin York. Born in a two-room cabin, the third of eleven children, York had almost no formal schooling. He was twenty-nine years old when he was drafted into the Army. On October 8, 1918, his unit was ordered to infiltrate enemy lines and attack a network of German machine guns near Châtel-Chéhéry, France. When his commanding officer and several of his comrades went down, Corporal York crawled forward and began shooting the enemy gunners one by one. Out of rifle ammunition when six Germans charged him, he pulled his pistol and killed them all. By the end of the hours-long battle, York was credited with taking out thirty-five German machine guns and killing twenty-five enemy soldiers; he and the seven men still alive in his unit captured 132 Germans and marched them back to American lines.

By the time York, now a sergeant, received the Medal of Honor, word of his actions had made him one of the most famous men in the world overnight. When the troopship that brought him home from Europe docked in New York in 1919, he was mobbed by reporters and fans. His newfound fame put him in a league with Henry Ford, Babe Ruth, and other heroes of the day.

World War II

The big question on the day after the Japanese attack on Pearl Harbor on December 7, 1941, was whether American boys from farms and small towns and big-city neighborhoods would be any match for the well-trained troops of Germany and Japan. By the end of the war, the answer was a clear yes: More than thirteen million Americans in uniform had suffered nearly one million casualties while fighting and winning wars in two regions—Europe and the Pacific—that were oceans and continents apart. The price they paid was shown not only by the 471 Medals of

Honor awarded during this war, but also by the fact that more than 270 of these were awarded posthumously.

Some medal recipients would become national heroes. Audie Murphy, for instance, at five feet five inches and 110 pounds, was at first turned down by the Marines, the Navy, and the Army when he tried to enlist because of his slight build. (He was also seventeen and tried to lie about his age.) When he was finally accepted by the Army, he was made a cook, but he insisted on joining a combat unit. By early 1945, he had risen to the rank of lieutenant as a result of battlefield promotions, received the Medal of Honor, and become one of the most decorated soldiers of the war, credited with personally killing 240 of the enemy. The news coverage he received helped turn him into a movie star in the 1950s.

Korea

The Korean War was called a police action because U.S. soldiers fought under the command of the United Nations and the U.S. government never formally declared war on the enemy. Although fought for reasons many Americans didn't fully understand, in a place about which they knew very little, the Korean War was a conflict in which the Medal of Honor shone brightly. Of the 145 medals awarded in Korea, nearly three-quarters of them were to men who didn't come home, one of the highest ratios of posthumous recipients of any war.

Vietnam

Unlike the Korean War, which much of the American public tried to ignore, the war in Vietnam was fought on the nightly television news and occasionally in the streets of America, as well as in the jungles of Southeast Asia. While GIs in World War II had been confident that the American public was firmly behind them, the soldiers of Vietnam, by comparison, felt that many of the people back home, deeply divided by the war, wished Vietnam would just go away. But these servicemen, the last to be drafted into military service, fought with great heroism—some because they believed in the mission, most simply because they didn't want to let the men next to them down.

The Medal of Honor was never tarnished by the controversy that surrounded the war in Vietnam. In fact, as the national mood shifted over time to an appreciation of the sacrifice that had taken place in the far-off jungles of that conflict, the medal and what it meant helped light the veterans' way back home to the admiration of their countrymen.

The history of the Medal of Honor became an issue at the end of the twentieth century and the dawning of the twenty-first. It came to light that the distinguished service of some soldiers in earlier wars had been overlooked as a result of social prejudices that existed in America at the time.

Acknowledging that the medal is about truth as well as courage, the Department of Defense looked back in its history to correct these mistakes. In 1997, medals were retroactively awarded to seven African American servicemen for gallantry in World War II. (Only one of them, Vernon Baker, whose story is recounted in this book, was still living.) In 2000, medals were awarded to twenty-two Asian Americans—seven of them still alive—whose bravery in World War II had never been fully recognized. In 2014, as a result of a review ordered by Congress, medals were awarded to twenty-four minority soldiers from World War II, Korea, and Vietnam whose heroic actions had been overlooked as a result of prejudice.

Iraq, Afghanistan, and the Continuing Fight Against Terrorism

The conventional wars in which our country fielded massive armies of citizen soldiers have become a thing of the past, as have the large-scale military engagements that resulted in great sacrifice and the awarding of many medals. Over the past three decades, American servicemen and women have seen combat in such varied and faraway places as Grenada, Panama, Bosnia, Kuwait (the Gulf War), and Somalia—fighting with higher-tech weapons in operations that lack the drama of past wars and sometimes escape public notice. Between 1975 (the end of the Vietnam War) and 2005, there were only two medals awarded, both posthumously: to Randy Schugart and Gary Gordon, members of the Army's Delta Force who went to the rescue of a downed helicopter pilot in the 1993 Battle of Mogidishu (as recounted in the book and movie *Black Hawk Down*) even though they knew they would probably not survive.

But bravery didn't stop when U.S. servicemen and women became an all-volunteer force involved in "low-grade" conflicts with "insurgents." In the war against terrorism that followed the attacks of 9/11, America's military answered the call with the valor it had displayed in previous wars. Volunteers flooded recruitment centers all over the country. The numbers tell a story of patriotism: Since the United States went to war in Afghanistan in 2001 and in Iraq two years later, more than 2.5 million members of the Army, Navy, Marine Corps, Air Force, and Coast Guard, and members of the reserves and National Guard, have served. Of these, more than a third have served more than one tour of duty in the battle zones. More than 6,600 of them have given their lives.

As of this writing, seventeen medals have been awarded for actions in Iraq and Afghanistan, seven of them posthumously, as battles in places such as Fallujah and the Korengal Valley take their place alongside the battles on Normandy Beach, Iwo Jima, and in the Chosin Reservoir. Like the men who had been awarded the medal before them, these Medal of Honor recipients wouldn't have been thought less of by their comrades if they had chosen not to act with such extreme bravery. But for reasons sometimes beyond our understanding—reasons having a great deal to do with duty, country, and honor, and almost nothing to do with the pursuit of fame and glory—they decided to look unflinchingly into the face of death and do the right thing.

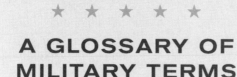

A GLOSSARY OF MILITARY TERMS

A-4E Skyhawk. A single-engine jet fighter bomber used by the U.S. Navy and Marine Corps during the Vietnam War, where it flew more missions than any other Navy aircraft.

AK-47. An automatic or semiautomatic rifle, powered by gas, with its ammunition fed from a magazine. It was invented in 1947 by Soviet engineer Mikhail Kalashnikov.

Ammunition clip. A case that holds ammunition and feeds it into the chamber of a firearm.

Anti-aircraft. Any weaponry (including guns and missiles) whose purpose is to defend against attacks from the air.

Apache helicopter. A U.S. Army attack helicopter equipped with guns, missiles, and rockets. Fast-moving and precise, it is used to strike targets from the air.

Armor. Material used to protect personnel and equipment from enemy fire. Ground forces with many personnel carriers and tanks are formed into armored units.

Army Special Forces. Soldiers trained in unconventional warfare and counterinsurgency tactics. They usually work in small units to train local forces or conduct secret missions. Known as the Green Berets during the Vietnam War, Special Forces trained and advised the South Vietnamese Army.

AWOL. Stands for "absent without leave." Any soldier who has left his post without permission is AWOL and faces charges for disobedience.

Basic training. The course that new recruits go through to become soldiers and prepare for battle.

Battery. A set of artillery guns or rocket launchers, generally of the same size or caliber. The typical artillery battery has about six artillery tubes or guns, plus communication equipment, ammunition, and vehicles. It includes from seventy to one hundred soldiers and one commanding officer.

Beehive darts. A type of ammunition, in the form of small steel barbs, discharged from a 105mm artillery shell. Beehive darts were fired against enemy ground troops during the Vietnam War.

Bunker. A heavily fortified hideout, often built of concrete, where soldiers and leaders can be protected from enemy fire.

Carbine. A short, lightweight, .30-caliber shoulder weapon used during World War II, Korea, and Vietnam.

Conscientious objector. A citizen who refuses to fight in war because of religious beliefs or a strong moral objection to taking the lives of others.

Counterinsurgency. A tactic to work with the local population, through training and alliances, to help them stand up to rebel forces (insurgents) and restore law and order.

Court-martial. The justice system used by the military to put on trial soldiers accused of disobedience and wrongdoing.

Dog tag. An identification tag worn by soldiers, usually attached to a chain worn around the neck.

DMZ. Abbreviation for "demilitarized zone," an area where no military activities are allowed, as agreed upon by both sides in the conflict. In many cases, the DMZ is a buffer zone between two territories that are at war.

F-100 Super Sabre jet (F-100). An Air Force jet fighter aircraft used in the Vietnam War. It was the first U.S. Air Force fighter plane able to fly faster than the speed of sound (supersonic) in level flight.

F-105 Thunderchief. A supersonic fighter-bomber used by the Air Force in Vietnam. A two-seat version called the "Wild Weasel" was used to suppress enemy air defenses.

F4U Corsair. An American fighter-bomber plane used in World War II and the Korean War, it was developed to launch from aircraft carriers.

Flak jacket. A form of body armor, often containing metal plates, that protects soldiers from sharp, dangerous objects ("flak") that result from exploding grenades and artillery shells.

Forward operating base (FOB). A fortified base set up in the field to reinforce military operations. It may include an airfield, a hospital, barracks, and other facilities to support soldiers and offer them a safe retreat if necessary.

Foxhole. A pit dug in the ground to provide protection from enemy fire.

F-84 Thunderjet. A fighter-bomber aircraft used by the U.S. Air Force in the Korean War. It was the first fighter aircraft to be able to refuel while in flight, and the first to carry a nuclear weapon.

GI. A member of the U.S. armed forces, "GI" is an abbreviation for "government issue." During World War II, the term "GI Joe" became the general nickname for all American servicemen.

Green Berets. Another name for U.S. Army Special Forces, an elite unit of soldiers that engages in special missions and operations such as search and rescue, training and supporting foreign fighters, and counterterrorism.

Grenade. A small explosive/projectile filled with explosive material or gas. Grenades are launched either by hand or projected through a large gun.

Gunship. A helicopter or fixed-wing aircraft, normally armed with light rockets or other large-caliber weapons.

Hanoi Hilton. The nickname for Hỏa Lò Prison near Hanoi, the capital of North Vietnam, where some of the American prisoners of war were held, interrogated, and tortured during the Vietnam War.

Howitzer. A type of artillery, towed or self-propelled, that fires shells of various sizes at medium speed and a relatively high trajectory.

Humvee. A heavily armored, four-wheel-drive vehicle used by the military. The name is from the acronym HMMWV, which stands for "high mobility multipurpose wheeled vehicle."

Medical Corps. A branch of the U.S. Army that includes trained doctors, nurses, and combat medics who can provide medical and surgical treatment to wounded soldiers.

Minefield. An area on land or in water that has been planted with encased explosives, or mines, which will blow up when stepped on or otherwise disturbed.

Mortar. A small muzzle-loading weapon that looks like a tube and fires shells at relatively short range with a high trajectory. Mortars are usually light and easy to take apart and carry from one place to another.

Navy SEAL. A specially trained unit of the U.S. Navy whose members, working in small teams, conduct military missions in rivers, lakes, oceans, and along coastlines, often in areas too shallow for submarines and ships to navigate. The name is an acronym for "sea, air, and land."

North Vietnamese Army (NVA). Officially known as the People's Army of North Vietnam. The troops were well trained and equipped, and they infiltrated South Vietnam by bicycle, truck, and foot.

Officer Candidate School (OCS). Training school for officers who did not attend a military academy or the Reserve Officer Training Corps (ROTC) program in college.

Pillbox. A small, low fortification that houses machine guns, antitank weapons, and other firearms, and the crew to operate them. Pillboxes are usually made of concrete, steel, or sandbags and then often covered by earth.

POW. An acronym for "prisoner of war."

Ranger. A soldier rigorously trained in raiding tactics, long-range patrols, and intelligence gathering.

Recoilless rifle. A light infantry cannon with holes in the rear of the barrel to allow propellant gases to escape. Because it fires at a slower speed, it has a shorter range than other guns. It is often used as an antitank weapon, and it can be fired from a ground mount or a vehicle.

Reconnaissance. A mission to get information that would be useful for offensive and defensive strategies, including the location and activities of the enemy and the physical features of the surrounding area.

Roadside bomb. A bomb hidden at the side of the road, sometimes set off remotely, designed to explode if run over by a passing vehicle. In Iraq and Afghanistan, these were referred to as "improvised explosive devices" (IEDs).

Rocket. A tubelike shell with various warheads that are forced out by gases or chemical reactions within the device.

Rocket launcher. A weapon capable of launching a rocket using gas or chemical reactions. Some of these are portable and can be operated by one individual.

Rocket-propelled grenade (RPG). A weapon fired from the shoulder capable of launching grenades. RPGs were first developed by the Soviet Union.

Round. The term used for a shot fired from a gun; also refers to the ammunition used in one shot from a weapon.

Shrapnel. Small fragments of an exploded bomb, shell, or grenade that can injure or kill anyone within range.

Sniper. A person who attacks the enemy by firing a rifle or other gun from a concealed position.

Special Forces. See Green Berets.

Strafe. To fire at people on the ground using automatic weapons from a low-flying airplane.

Surface-to-air missiles (SAMs). Surface-launched missiles of various sizes, ranges, and heights used against targets in the air. Fighter aircraft are usually able to outmaneuver these missiles if they see them in time.

Tommy gun. Nickname for the Thompson submachine gun (named after inventor General John T. Thompson), a handheld rapid-firing machine gun used in World War II.

Wingman. The second aircraft in a flight formation. The wingman's role is to defend the flight leader, particularly from attacks from the rear.

★ AUTHOR'S NOTE ★

Nick Kehoe's name should appear on the cover of this book as its co-author. He has lent his good counsel and strong insights to this project at every step of the way since it began. But typically he not only sought no credit but actively refused it. However much he may downplay his role, though, *I* know how crucial he has been in getting *Choosing Courage* done and how lucky I have been to have the pleasure of his company during its completion.

I want to thank the David Horowitz Freedom Center, where I work, for establishing a context for this book. And my old friend Wally Nunn, who helped make *Choosing Courage* happen, as he has other good things. Thanks as well to Tom Wilkerson and Ron Rand of the Medal of Honor Foundation for seeing value in this project. And of course thanks, too, to the heroes whose stories are told here. They reinforce the old lesson: We are the land of the free only because we are also the home of the brave.

Thanks to Ann Bramson of Artisan Books, who was present in every way at the creation of this book. To Laurie Orseck, whose resourcefulness, patience, and deft editorial touch were decisive in shaping the final product. And to Lelia Mander for getting the manuscript over all the hurdles that lead to the printing press, and Kara Strubel for her compelling art direction.

I see this book as a kiss for my wife, Mary Jo, and hope it will be an inspiration for the Collier grandchildren—Eden Guthrie, James Wyeth, Mercy Josephine, and Peter William—all of them lights of my life.

INDEX

Note: Page numbers in *italics* refer to illustrations.

Germany
  and Holocaust, 4, 48–50, *51*, 52–53
  and World War II, 1–4
  See also World War II
Giunta, Salvatore, 134–41, *135*, *141*
Gordon, Gary, 210
Great Britain, 1
Guadalcanal, battle of, 4, 65

H

Haffey, Neil, 100
Haiti, *195*, 196–97
Hall of Heroes in the Pentagon, 170
Hambleton, Iceal "Gene," 118–22, *121*, 127
Hanoi Hilton, 108–9, *109*
  and Day, 105–7, 108
  and Thorsness, 112–16, *115*, *116*
Hawk, John, 204
Hess, Kendra, 185
Higgins, Daniel, 162, 163
Hill, Dan, 178, 181
Hillel, 201
Hirohito, Emperor of Japan, 4
Hiroshima, Japan, 4
Hitler, Adolf, 1, 3, 48, 52
Ho Chi Minh, 79
Holloway, Gwendell, 89, 91, 92
Holocaust, 4, 48–50, *51*, 52–53
Hoppes, Jonna Doolittle, 14–19, *19*
Howard, Robert, *181*
howitzers, *62*, *83*, 83–84, 213
Hudner, Tom, 70–77, *71*

Hungary, 48–49, *51*, 52–53
Hurricane Isaac, 174
Hussein, Saddam, 131–32

I

I Could Never Be So Lucky Again (Doolittle), 18
Ia Drang, battle of, 177
IEDs (improvised explosive devices), 164, 214
integration of U.S. military, 42–43
internment of Japanese Americans, 20–21, *27*, 27–28, *28*
Iraq
  and Dunham, 167–71
  and Islamic State (ISIS), 132
  and Milligan, 152–55, *154*
  and posthumously awarded Medals of Honor, 206, 210
  and Rascon, 100
  and Romesha, 147
  and search for weapons of mass destruction, 131–32
  and the Taliban, 143
Islamic State (ISIS), 132–33
Italy, *xiv*, 1, 3
Ivory Coast, 193
Iwo Jima, battle of, *9*, 9
  casualties of, *10*
  and Lucas, 5, *8*, 8, 10, 11

J

Jacobs, Jack, xii, *xii*, 174, 199–202, *200*, *201*
Japan and World War II, 1–4, *4*, 9, *9*

on fear, 68

and internment of Japanese Americans, 21

on intervention in World War II, 2

Roosevelt, Theodore, Sr., 205

Roosevelt, Theodore, Jr., 205

Rosser, Richard, 58, 63

Rosser, Ronald, 57–63, *58, 60, 63*

Rubin, Tibor, 48–51, *49,* 54, 55–56, *56,* 203

Rwandan genocide, 198

S

Sagami, Yoheie, 23

Sakato, George, 20–26, *21, 25*

San Juan Hill, battle of, 205

Sandy Hook Elementary School, 173

Saudi Arabia, 183

Schugart, Randy, 210

Seabees, *43*

SEALs (Sea, Air, and Land teams)

and bin Laden, 131, *183*

Norris and Thornton, 117–27

training regimen, *128,* 128–29, *129*

in Vietnam, 117–27, *125*

September 11th, 2001 terrorist attacks, 182–83

and campaigns in Afghanistan and Iraq, 131–32

and Giunta, 134, 135–36

heroism exhibited after, 210

Jacobs on, 201

on Pentagon, *183,* 183

and Rascon, 100

and Rescorla, 175

on World Trade Center, 178–81, *179, 182,* 182–83

Seventh-Day Adventists, 29, 32

Shaffer, Jesse, III, 174

Shaffer, Jesse, IV, 174

Sharia (Islamic law), 142

Silver Star Award recipients

Jacobs, *201*

Rescorla, 177

"sole survivor" policy, 65

Soviet Union

and Cold War, 45

and the Taliban, 142, *143*

and World War II, 1, 3–4

Spanish American War, 205

Star of David, *52, 53*

Stockdale, James, 109, *110,* 110

Stotts, Connor, 173

Sullivan, Al, *64,* 64–65

Sullivan, Frank, *64,* 64–65

Sullivan, George, *64,* 64–65

Sullivan, Joe, *64,* 64–65

Sullivan, Matt, *64,* 64–65

T

Taliban, 142–43

in Afghanistan, 132, 142–43, 144–45, *150*

and bin Laden, 131

and Giunta, 137–40

and Outpost Keating, 144–45

and Lynch, *189*, 190–92

and Medals of Honor awarded to overlooked soldiers, 209

and Navy SEALs, 117–27, *125*

and Norris, 117–27

and paratroopers, 67–68, *69*

and posthumously awarded Medals of Honor, 206

prisoners of war in, 103–8, 108–9, 112–16

protests against, 80, *81*, 208

and Rascon, 94–97, 100

and Rescorla, 176, 177

rocket launchers used in, *81*

and Thornton, 117–27

and Thorsness, 111–16

W

Walker, Mary, 205

Walter Reed National Military Medical Center, 155

war on terror, 133

weapons of mass destruction, 131–32

Wise, Beau, 65

Wise, Ben, 65

Wise, Jeremy, 65

women
as Medal of Honor recipients, 205
and World War II, *3*, 3

World Trade Center, 178–81, *179*, *182*, 182–83

World War I, 206–7

World War II, 1–4

African Americans in, *xiv*, 36, 37–38, 40–41, *42*, *43*

aircraft carriers in, *4*

Allied forces, *1*, 1–4, 53

Axis forces, 1, 3

and Baker, 36–41

and Castle Aghinolfi assault, 39–40

civilian casualties in, 204

civilians' contributions to, 2–3, *3*

and Day, 101

and Doolittle, 14–19, *15*, *16*, *17*

and Doss, 29–35

and Guadalcanal, 4, 65

and Holocaust, 4, 48–49, *51*, 52–53

and Iwo Jima, 4, 9, *9*, *10*

Jacobs on, 201

and Japanese Americans, 20–21, 209

and Lucas, 5–11, 12

and Medals of Honor awarded to overlooked soldiers, 209

and Murphy, 207–8

and Okinawa, 4, 31–35, *32*, *34*

and Pearl Harbor, *2*, 2, 6, *16*, *23*, 29

and posthumously awarded Medals of Honor, 206, 207

and Roosevelt, Jr., 205

and Sakato, 20–26

and the Sullivan Brothers, *64*, 64–65

Y

York, Alvin, 207

youngest soldiers, 12–13, *13*

PHOTOGRAPHY CREDITS

Fotosearch RM /age fotostock america, Inc. p. 182; **AP/ Wide World Photos:** pgs. 47, 62, 69, 81, 85, Maya Alleruzzo p. 154, Peter Arnett p. 176, FS p. 28 (left), Eileen Hillock p. 178, National Park Service p. 27, Dang Van Phuoc p. 78, U.S. Marine Corps p. 32, U.S. Navy pgs. 15, 23, Nick Ut p. 121, Ted S. Warren p. 165; **Getty Images**: U.S. Navy/Authenticated News p. 125, Juan Barreto/AFP p. 195, Doug Kanter/AFP p. 179 (bottom), Stephen Jaffee/AFP p. 183 (top), National Archives/AFP p. 91, Blank Archives p. 80, Buyenlarge p. 28 (right), Fotosearch pgs. 1, 13, Otto Greule Jr. 165 (bottom), Fine Art Images/Heritage Images p. 52, Jewish Chronicle/Heritage Images p. 53, Hulton Archive p. 16, Miguel Salmeron/The Image Bank p. 129, Interim Archives p. 43, Office of War Information/Interim Archives p. 64, Alan Radecki/U.S. Navy/Northrop Grumman p. 133, David Hume Kennerly p. 110, Joe McNally p. 128, MPI p. 3, Susan Watts/*NY Daily News* Archive 179 (top), Scott Olson 165 (top), Photo Quest pgs. xiv, 39, 44, 104, Rolls Press/Popperfoto pgs. 98, 191, Express/Stringer p. 2, Alfred Eisenstaedt/The LIFE Picture Collection p. 99, Louis R. Lowery/U.S. Marine Corps/The LIFE Picture Collection p. 10, Time Life Pictures/U.S. Air Force/The LIFE Picture Collection p. 17, W. Eugene Smith/Time Life Pictures pgs. 4, 34, Gabriel Benzur/Time & Life Pictures p. 42, Sovfoto/UIG p. 46, Universal History Archive pgs. 51, 183 (bottom); **National Archive Collection** p. 31; **Tim Page** p. 97; **Reuters**: Erik De Castro p. 150, Handout p. 109, Adrees Latif p. 130 (bottom), Stringer Afghanistan p. 143, Tim Wimborne p. 130 (top). **All other photographs courtesy of the Congressional Medal of Honor Foundation.**